# *Between Faith and Tears*

*by*
*Kenneth E. Schemmer, M.D.*

Copyright © 2012 by Kenneth E. Schemmer, M.D.

*Between Faith and Tears*
by Kenneth E. Schemmer, M.D.

Printed in the United States of America

ISBN 9781622308262

All rights reserved solely by the author. The author guarantees all contents are original and do not infringe upon the legal rights of any other person or work. No part of this book may be reproduced in any form without the permission of the author. The views expressed in this book are not necessarily those of the publisher.

Unless otherwise indicated, Bible quotations are taken from the Revised Standard Version. Copyright © 1946, 1952, 1971, 1973.

Verses marked KJV are from the King James Version of the Bible.

Verses marked NEB are from the New English Bible. Copyright © The Delegates of the Oxford University Press and the Syndics of the Cambridge University Press 1961, 1970. Reprinted by permission.

Verses marked NIV are from the Holy Bible: New International Version. Copyright © 1978 by the New York International Bible Society. Used by permission of Zondervan Bible Publishers.

Verses marked NKJB_NT in this publication are from The New King James Bible-New Testament. Copyright © 1979, Thomas Nelson, Inc. Publishers.

www.xulonpress.com

## ACKNOWLEDGMENTS

To the many patients who have allowed me to share the tragedies and triumphs of their bodies and souls.

To the professors of Anderson School of Theology, Anderson, Indiana, who helped me clarify my thoughts and concepts: Dr. John M. Vayhinger, Dr. Barry L. Callen, Dr. Gene W. Newberry, Dr. Adam W. Miller, Mr. Fred Shively, and Dr. James Earl Massey.

To Dr. Harold L. Phillips, former editor of *Vital Christianity*, who reviewed concepts of healing and wholeness expressed throughout church history.

To Dr. Kenneth F. Hall, who gave guidance and direction in the development of this book.

To Laura Withrow and Kay Shively for editorial assistance.

To Rev. R. Eugene Sterner and Dr. Milton A. Buettner for encouragement and review of part of this work.

To Florene Prunty, Judy Tiesel, Marilyn Palumbo, and Rhonda Neidert for typing assistance.

To my wife for her encouragement; many hours of listening to rough drafts; frequent, perceptive, and fitting suggestions; and willingness to let me take time to write this book.

To my four children, Karla, Kenny, Kay, and Kami, for their understanding attitude when the demands of writing interfered with the duties of their dad.

To Helen Hosier, my editor at Thomas Nelson Publishers, for her invaluable contribution to this book.

*To the glory
of our Lord and Savior Jesus Christ
who, through my mother and father,
taught me in the daily struggles of life
many of the concepts expressed
in this book.*

# CONTENTS

Foreword ................................ vii
Introduction ............................. 11
1 Sharing in God's Healing Ministry ............ 13

### PART ONE
*Six Personal Histories*

2 Kay Lynne ............................. 25
3 Keri .................................. 32
4 Keith ................................. 43
5 Lawrence .............................. 50
6 Paul .................................. 57
7 Ellen ................................. 71

### PART TWO
*A Doctor's View of Healing*

8 The Miracle of Wholeness ................. 85
9 Is There Meaning in Suffering? ........... 101
10 The Struggle for Faith .................. 111
11 From Here to Eternity: A Conclusion ..... 123
   Notes ................................ 130

# FOREWORD

This is a personal book—about people's lives and your life. This is not a "success" book, or a "how-to-do-it" book, but a "think" book. I like this book, because it is both human and honest. Kenneth Schemmer asks you to think, reflect, and evaluate.

What is the basic issue here? The dark experiences of life: accident, sickness, failure, despair, fear, frustration, pain, suffering, loss, misery, hurt, crippling, impotence, helplessness.

What are some of the common answers to these experiences most of us encounter—answers we find that are no answers at all?

- The game of let's pretend—it won't happen to us.
- The Pollyana attitude. There must be a silver lining of blessing in every cloud.
- A stoic philosophy. Tough it out with a stiff upper lip, and we will survive.
- The epicurean philosophy. Forget it. Eat, drink, and be merry for tomorrow we all die.
- Existential absurdity. There is no meaning or value. God is dead, and the only question is whether we should live or die.
- Rational materialism. Medical technology offers "better living through chemistry," and soon medical science will find the cure for death!

- Religious animism. God can be manipulated like a human being. Magical miracles can be wrought by penance, sacrifice, or emotional persuasion.

Dr. Schemmer is quite candid in exposing the non-Christian quality of each of the above answers. In contrast he offers a thoroughly biblical understanding of sickness, pain, and suffering. Are there Christian answers? Yes, says Dr. Schemmer. But the answers are not always easy.

I want to note the major themes of the Christian response, so that the reader may trace the importance of each biblical emphasis throughout the book.

The Bible does not ignore the dark experiences of life but places them squarely in the center of life.

It is better to go to a house of mourning than to go to a house of feasting, for death is the destiny of every man; the living should take this to heart. Sorrow is better than laughter, because a sad face is good for the heart (Eccl. 7:2,3 NIV).

We are not admonished to be morose, morbid, or masochistic. But rather, if we fear death and attempt to avoid death, then we will spend our entire lives avoiding the dark experiences and will never live!

"Whoever tries to keep his life will lose it, and whoever loses his life will preserve it" (Luke 17:33 NIV).

Second, we are part of a fallen creation. Our bodies are part of that fallen creation. Accident, misfortune, sickness, and death are the inevitable consequences for us all. Therefore, all Christians will experience the painful dark consequences. It is not God's purpose that His children should suffer pain, misery, and misfortune—but we will not escape the contamination of fallen creatureliness.

"As was the earthly man, so are those who are of the earth; and as is the man from heaven, so also are those who are of heaven" (1 Cor. 15:48 NIV).

Third, just as our physical body is of corrupt dust, so is our psychological self. We need not be victimized by our dark experiences; we can have victory in and through Christ. But a word of caution. Victory does not mean the elimination of emotional anguish, pain, and hurt. It does not mean that we will always have good, right feelings or thoughts. Rather, victory over our dark experiences in the Christian sense is to affirm and proclaim our wholeness in Christ. We need to be "always giving thanks to God the Father for everything. . ." (Eph. 5:20 NIV) and to claim the promise that ". . . in all things God works for the good of those who love him . . ." (Rom. 8:28 NIV).

> E. Mansell Pattison, M.D.
> Chairman, Department of Psychiatry
> Medical College of Georgia, Augusta

# INTRODUCTION

"Doctor, I just can't understand why I'm sick. I didn't ask to be ill, and I don't like it. Please help me get well quickly. This suffering bit has no value anyway."

Patients often say such things. As a young doctor I thought I should help people get over illness as quickly as possible so it would have minimal effect on them. Over the past twenty years, however, I have had many patients who were able to find meaning in their suffering. Some commented on how much they grew as persons through their sickness. Some who suffered for years with incurable, chronic diseases still displayed peace and joy.

As a Christian physician, I would like to talk with you in this book about transcending tragedy when it strikes you personally or when it visits those you love. I want you to walk in the shoes of six patients who have faced tragedy and won. I have become convinced that we can do more than merely "cope" with trials and sufferings. Going beyond such problems requires a faith that allows us to grow and mature. How we relate to God and how He relates to us in the tragedies of life are at the heart of the discussion. Through faith in Jesus Christ, I believe we can find the resources to overcome whatever tragedies life brings us.

The material in this book lends itself either to group discussion or to private devotions.

All chapters conclude with a section called *For Discussion*. The questions will help you rethink what you have just read, especially if you write out your thoughts in a notebook.

# CHAPTER 1
## Sharing in God's Healing Ministry

In 1959 I started my medical training because I felt God calling me to serve Him as a physician. At that time I perceived the practice of medicine as the ultimate way to share in God's healing ministry. During succeeding years of training, I gained knowledge and skills to "help God" wherever He wanted me to.

Before my training was completed, I encountered hundreds of patients. I saw how much many of them suffered and how often they carried the burdens of their tragic situations on their own shoulders. I wondered how their diseases affected their total personalities.

I began to ask: What is the meaning of suffering? Is it even worth being human if humans have to go through such tragedies? My personal experience soon provided grist for the mill of my soul.

In early 1963 my wife Karrol became pregnant. We were thrilled and delighted, but after three months of a normal pregnancy the doctor told her that her uterus was not as big as it should be. A repeat pregnancy test was positive. The next week, however, she began to bleed and feel abdominal pain. She was forced to stop teaching and stay in bed for a week. Then, on Mother's Day, 1963, her doctor removed a dead, degenerated fetus.

Eighteen months later in October 1964, Karrol delivered our first baby, Karla Jean. At Karla's six-week checkup the doctor found that she had a congenital dislocation of the left hip. She wore a brace for six months to correct it.

Our second child was a son, Kenny. In October 1967, Karrol delivered our third child, Kay Lynne, who almost died in her first twenty-four hours of life. Her story will be told in Chapter 2.

In November 1967, my dad's chronic abnormal heartbeat was severely aggravated by a bleeding ulcer produced by medicine he took for arthritis. His heart began to beat over two hundred times a minute. Despite the use of heart medications, his heartbeat could not be controlled. The doctor shocked his heart with an electric current, but my dad almost died before we could get his heart to beat again. In 1969 my mother had a hysterectomy to remove a cancer of the uterus. Because it was diagnosed early, the operation was a success.

In November 1970, Kenny, then four years old, fell head-first down the clothes chute. He landed on the cement basement floor and fractured his skull.

*Closer to Home*

In early 1972, when I got sick, I was ripe for a deeper understanding of suffering. One early January morning, abdominal pain, vomiting, and diarrhea suddenly struck me. At first I assumed that those symptoms indicated only a minor abdominal illness. Although the vomiting and diarrhea subsided in nine hours, the pain continued. As a doctor, I wondered why I was sick. The next day my skin and eyes turned yellow. I had a diseased gall bladder and a gallstone in my bile duct.

As a Christian, I felt troubled in spirit. The pain and weakness confused and stunned me spiritually. I felt as if death were hovering over me. How can I handle this suffering if it gets any worse or doesn't let up soon? I questioned. My prayers became more serious as I talked with God about my sickness: "Lord, I don't like to feel this horrible, and I want to get well. But there must be some reason for suffering. I want to draw closer to You if I can."

As a Christian I wanted not to deny my agony but to face my problem squarely. I believed God's promise, ". . .'I will never fail you nor forsake you' " (Heb. 13:5). I asked God to give me the courage I needed to accept my suffering. I asked for the peace and joy in my soul that others needed to see in me in order to know He was still with me.

Then the tiredness started. Fatigue overcame me. Walking to and from the bathroom wore me out so much that I would sleep for hours. While the disease progressed, I questioned my motives. Which concerned me more: My health and my work as a surgeon or my relationship with Christ? I had asked that question before, but now I needed to express my love for Him, even if I would never be able to operate again.

Would God miraculously heal me, or did He want to work through His natural laws of healing and through physicians? I felt peace flooding my soul. Either I would be delivered from this suffering quickly, or He would use my suffering to help me grow as a person.

When my five-hour operation ended, I experienced the most severe physical pain of my life. I couldn't believe anything could hurt so much. I cried out, "God, where on earth are You? Why does there have to be such pain and suffering in this world?" Then I recalled that Jesus had asked the same question on the cross, yet He had suffered and died so that the love of God might be shared with humankind. Despite my shattered physical condition and stunned psyche, by faith I rose a bit above my misery.

Nevertheless, my struggle for complete faith in Jesus Christ continued. My whole life seemed to pass before me. I recalled my weaknesses when I had problems, and I remembered my sins. I grew discouraged as I fought this great spiritual battle. Was I going to give up on God or would I stake everything in faith on Jesus Christ? Would He keep what I had committed to Him, even through this suffering? Finally, I chose to trust myself to Christ Jesus—body, mind, and soul.

During the first five days after my operation, pain and weakness wore me out. My roommate was dying with cancer of the lung. Most of those nights he coughed excessively, trying to breathe. Each time I fell asleep, his coughing woke me. During those desperate attempts to gain his breath, he wanted me to talk to him and reassure him that he would not die before his wife came in the morning. Consequently I felt so tired during the day that I had to push myself to pray for others, read the Bible, and commune with Christ.

*Ultimate Trust*

Despite my physical fatigue and emotional exhaustion, Jesus gave me a peace and joy that convinced me I still had an authentic spiritual life. He had sustained my commitment to Him after all. Now I knew I could trust Him even in death.

Eventually I began to recover. Each day as I gained new strength, my faith in Jesus Christ increased. I yearned to spend my time and my life for Him.

"Lord Jesus," I prayed, "I accept my situation in health or sickness and depend on You to give me wholeness. From now on I dedicate my energies to serving You. In sickness I trust You with my weaknesses and ask for energy to handle my illness. Show Your presence in my life that I might share You, whether I'm healed physically or not."

As others worked or visited with me, His spirit enlivened our relationships with fruit: love and joy, peace and forgiveness, kindness and gentleness, patience, faithfulness, and self-control.

One month after the operation I returned to my surgical training program. I had new sensitivity to the needs of my patients. Now I could anticipate many of their physical, emotional, and spiritual needs. I met those needs best when I listened to their struggles and told them about mine. I discovered the importance of treating the whole patient, not just the body. As I communicated with my patients, people began to tell me what meaning and value they were finding in their suffering.

At first my sickness had appeared to be an impediment to my growth as a surgeon. When I found out I would lose at least two months' experience as chief resident, I had despaired. But the Lord knew I needed those months to gain new insights. Had God miraculously healed me, I would have lost only two weeks. A supernatural healing would have increased my faith in Him. That kind of increase in faith, however, could not be compared to the confidence in Him I had gained by going through such agony myself.

Not only can I now trust Him even in the face of death, but I have found that true healing extends beyond the body to the patient's personhood. I can share in Christ's healing ministry by sharing His Spirit with my patients.

This sharing of Christ in our relationships was described by the apostle Paul in 2 Corinthians 5:18–20:

> All this is from God, who through Christ reconciled us to himself and gave us the ministry of reconciliation; that is, God was

in Christ reconciling the world to himself, not counting their trespasses against them, and entrusting to us the message of reconciliation. So we are ambassadors for Christ, God making his appeal through us. . . .

### Strength to Transcend

By faith in Jesus Christ we can find the resources to transcend tragedy. What are those resources that will help us go beyond our problems?

Our basic resource is the gift of the Spirit of Christ which God gives us. When the Holy Spirit dwells in us, He guides the maturing of our personality so that we can become the persons we are meant to be. Jesus Christ, God's Son, is the Mediator between the Father and us—and between us and others. Our interpersonal relationships then provide the love and caring that others need in order to grow despite suffering in their lives. We can be more authentic in our concern for others when we deepen our relationship with God as a result of our own experiences. What God does for me and with me, He wants to do through me. When I honestly share with others my weaknesses and sufferings and the way God had to work in me, others can gain insight and hope. As one patient said, "If God could help you, maybe He would help me."

### Why Do We Care?

One day I was attending to a patient with whom I had worked for two years. Suddenly he looked at me and said, "Why do you care so much for me? No one else has ever cared for me the way you do."

"Because that is the way God cares for me," I replied.

As we become vulnerable to others and actually share the love, peace, and joy that God gives us, they can receive help that is beyond our giving. And an amazing thing happens:

We find further healing for ourselves. We no longer need be so concerned about ourselves—our problems, suffering, and needs—but can concentrate on helping others.

After we receive Jesus Christ in our lives, we can converse with God the Father and commune with the Holy Spirit. We were created for that kind of communion. When the Holy Spirit cleanses our hearts and minds, we gain control of ourselves. Then He can begin to manifest Himself in our relationships with others.

As people see the fruit of the Spirit in our relationships with them, they can see the image of God in us. The Scriptures tell us that the "fruit of the Spirit is love, joy, peace, patience, kindness, goodness, faithfulness, gentleness, self-control . . ." (Gal. 5:22,23).

When we allow Christ to be the Mediator in our relationships with others, we put Him in the center of those relationships. His love controls us and enables us to see others as God does. We are all co-strugglers who need to know that God loves us even when the disappointments of life seem to indicate He has forsaken us. Viewed from this perspective, our compassion takes on purpose.

What we humans need, especially when we hurt, is fellowship with other human beings. Fellowship is not just superficial chatting; it is the in-depth sharing of our whole selves with each other. It is vulnerability, the opening of the inner me to the inner you. It is not a you-talk-and-I-listen session. It is the giving of ourselves to one another without ulterior motives or desires. Through fellowship, we encounter each other as human beings who are part of the same family. We compare our lives—the meanings we find, the problems we have. We come to understand each other in deeper ways.

It works that way for me. I can relax in Christ's affirmation of me without always having to be affirmed by others. Then, when I meet a person in need, I can control myself enough to allow the Holy Spirit to express Himself to the other person. I ask Christ what fruit of His abiding Spirit the person I am conversing with needs now. Then I ask Christ to share that fruit through me. It is not the specific words or answers we give our fellow sufferers, but the sharing of the Spirit of Christ in our interpersonal relationships that makes the difference.

*For Discussion*

1. Recount the worst sickness you have had. Did you question why you were sick? Did you wonder what you had done to allow such an affliction to overcome you?

2. If a severe disease should strike you down and not only prevent you from working but even confine you to a hospital room, how would you respond? When tragedy comes, what are the first thoughts that come to your mind? Denial? Anger? Depression? Are you worried and anxious?

3. What do you fear the most about being sick—loss of money, time, activity? Does the fear of death enter into your thoughts and behavior?

4. Do you perceive suffering as thoroughly negative, or can you see any value in discomfort? List the possible benefits and drawbacks of suffering.

5. Discuss how God can be glorified in our tragedies. Does God minister to suffering humanity today?

6. How do you conceive of God's healing ministry? How can human beings share in it?

7. How do you respond to the statement, "What God does for me and with me, He wants to do through me"?

8. What did Jesus mean when He said, ". . .'Father, into thy hands I commit my spirit!'. . ." (Luke 23:46)? Mention ideas and Scripture passages that clarify how we live when we put our spirits in God's hands.

9. How can we allow Jesus Christ to express Himself in our lives? Can we really share Him with others? In John 15 Jesus calls Himself the Vine and us the branches. We glorify the Father by bearing fruit. What fruits of our lives prove that Christ abides in us and we in Him?

# PART ONE

Six Personal Histories

# CHAPTER 2
## Kay Lynne

*Kay Lynne Schemmer, our second daughter, was born with serious health problems. It seemed hopeless. This is the story of what happened and the way God increased our faith.*

"Ken, you have a dead baby! It's just a matter of turning off the respirator." The words of the chief surgeon of Children's Hospital in Cincinnati, Ohio, pierced me like a dagger. "Even if we were to insert a tube into her chest to relieve pressure from the lungs, little would be accomplished. Her lungs have been almost totally digested by enzymes. They cannot expand."

This frightening situation occurred during my surgical residency. We had anticipated a routine delivery with our third child. Karrol had enjoyed a marvelous pregnancy with no illnesses, no injuries, no falls. On that October night in 1967, however, it was evident at the beginning of the birth process that an intrauterine mishap had occurred. As the membranes broke, dark, thick, green water flowed out. When Kay Lynne's head appeared, she was so discolored I could not even determine the color of her hair. Her skin was stained green. Otherwise she was a large, apparently strong baby, and all bodily systems initially tested perfect. Within five minutes of birth, however, we found her lungs seriously damaged by the intestinal enzymes she had breathed in during the delivery. Ten minutes later her skin turned from olive green to blue, head to toe, and it stayed that way even when pure oxygen was administered. The green water so saturated her lungs that all attempts failed to remove it completely. As a result, enzymatic digestion of the lung tissue continued unabated. Little Kay Lynne was in desperate trouble.

Five hours after her birth we transferred her to the newborn intensive care unit. She required intravenous fluids and drugs to neutralize the acid which the lungs could not remove from the blood. Twelve hours after birth her skin remained blue and her general condition continued to worsen. Eight medical specialists were consulted. Four said to give her antibiotics. The other four said that antibiotics could kill her. Four of the eight said steroids might help. The others said steroids could make her worse. No one knew what to do. Kay Lynne weakened hourly.

I returned to duty at General Hospital just across the street. An hour later I received an urgent call to return to Kay Lynne's bed. I cried as I ran back to Children's Hospital, then paused before entering the intensive care unit. Not knowing what to expect, I prayed for the strength and grace to handle whatever situation awaited me. I entered the room. There our baby lay, seemingly lifeless. A mechanical respirator was breathing for her, but her skin remained blue. I was crushed. I tried to hold back more tears.

As soon as the pediatrician saw my grief, he quietly told me what had happened.

### *No Hope*

The pediatric resident who had helped take care of Kay Lynne had returned to the intensive care unit because of a strangely uncomfortable feeling. He saw that Kay Lynne's skin had turned black and that she was not breathing. Immediately he gave her mouth-to-mouth resuscitation. A cardiologist put a needle in the right side of her chest, and air gushed out. Her right lung had ruptured.

In a few minutes she began to breathe again with assistance. Inserting a tube through her mouth and vocal cords into her windpipe, the doctor connected her to a respirator. From that point on, however, Kay Lynne appeared dead. She had no reflexes, her pupils would not react, and she lay motionless except for the rising of her chest as the respirator pumped pure oxygen into her severely damaged lungs.

Yet her heart continued to beat and her kidneys to function. Then, just as she seemed to stabilize, her right lung ruptured again. This time the respirator provided no help. An X-ray picture of Kay's chest showed the right lung collapsed, with air pushing both lungs far to the left side of the chest. There was air between the lungs and in the sac surrounding the heart. Her skin remained black, and she did not respond to various stimuli. I raised her arms and legs, but they fell limply to the bed.

I was in turmoil. We had been planning for over a year to have this child. Karla and Kenny had helped us set up a room for Kay Lynne. Even if her vital organs could be supported long enough for her lungs to heal, would she ever be able to think, talk, or play? How would I tell the older children? How would Karrol cope with Kay Lynne's death?

The chief surgeon checked Kay again. He told me gently that nothing could be accomplished by further treatment. "We could put a rubber tube in her chest to drain out the air that has collapsed her lung," he said, "but her lung is too digested and stiff to reexpand."

Was it time to give up? Should we accept our child's death? The knowledge of the devastating effect of insufficient oxygen to nourish her brain had tormented us for many hours. We certainly did not want our baby to live if she would be only a vegetable. As a surgical resident, I knew that the chief surgeon spoke the truth. The situation appeared hopeless. Yet, responding as a father, I requested that a rubber tube be inserted into her chest. The air trapped there again gushed out, and the respirator pumped more easily. Nothing else changed.

The surgeon suggested I go home and take care of Karla and Kenny. He offered to call me in a few hours when our baby died. Reluctant to leave, however, I lingered by Kay's plastic-covered bed. Tubes connected life-supporting devices to almost every opening in her body as well as to her blood vessels. From a medical viewpoint, Kay Lynne had died five hours ago. Only the respirator sustained any sign of life.

As I stood watching our baby, my soul trembled. A battle raged inside me. On the one hand, I wanted our baby to live, enjoy health, and run and play like other children. On the other hand, God seemed to be asking me if I were more concerned about Jesus Christ and His glory or about myself and the glory of a healthy baby girl. I looked again at that helpless little body. I struggled to understand this tragedy in the light of what I believed about God.

Then some words of Jesus came to my mind, " 'I, when I am lifted up . . . will draw all men to myself' " (John 12:32). How could Jesus be lifted up through the death of a child? I did not understand why God would want Kay Lynne's death, but I did understand that He wanted my love no matter what developed.

I surrendered my insufficient resources to the all-sufficient God. I bowed over our child and gave her to Him. I wanted God's will. Whether she lived or died, I would accept it.

When I opened my eyes again, I was electrified. I saw what seemed to be a resurrection. Our baby girl began to suck on the tube going to her windpipe. Her little legs began to move. As I watched in amazement, her skin became a warm pink. "Nurse, look!" I shouted. "The Lord is healing my baby! Please—call the technician to take another X-ray."

I examined the new X-ray pictures. Her lung had expanded, and the air around her heart was gone. We checked her blood again. The acidity, carbon dioxide, and oxygen registered within the normal range. A strong sense of peace filled my soul. I knew that our baby would be completely well.

The next morning the radiologist compared the improvement in Kay's chest X-ray with those taken the preceding night. He was astounded. Hour by hour Kay grew stronger. She sucked vigorously from the bottle, and she looked like a perfectly normal baby. Within thirty-six hours after God had healed her, the tube was removed from her windpipe. Eight days later the doctor released her.

That normal baby is today a bright, alert, teen-ager. The pediatrician who performs her routine checkups continues to marvel. As I watch her run and play or listen to her pray, I thank God for His Son who still, even in our sophisticated age, displays power to bring the dead back to life.

*Seeing Our Mission*
*Read John 12:20–28.*

In trying to understand how the suffering of a newborn baby could bring glory to God, John 12:20–28 seemed to be meaningful. For almost two thousand years, people have been asking to see the Son of God. Just as the disciples' mission was to bring people to Jesus, our mission today is to show people God's Son. Karrol and I tried to keep that mission predominant even in Kay Lynne's desperate situation.

In this scriptural account Karrol and I found the central theme of the cross: There is no life without death. If we are willing to die to selfishness, we ultimately win. We could have demanded that God give us our own way, healing our daughter's physical body. Understanding and wholeness came, however, when we became more concerned about Jesus Christ and His glory than about the death or life of our baby girl. Karrol and I asked for Jesus Christ to be lifted up so that all the people with whom we were associated might be drawn to Him. At that point of commitment, God healed our baby.

### Steps of Growth

Through this experience I learned several things:

1. God is able even in these times of great scientific achievement to accomplish what is beyond human ability and understanding.

2. God works in ways that are mysterious to us and that are not dependent on what we think or demand.

3. God works not only in the physical realm but within an individual's entire personality.

4. We often become so involved with God's creation that it assumes more importance to us than the Creator.

5. Not only was Kay's life restored, but I matured in my relationship with God—even before He healed her.

6. Everyone has been created for a purpose; although a baby might live for only a day, she or he may still fulfill that purpose.

7. Whether or not God healed Kay Lynne did not depend on me. If I had decided to terminate use of the respirator, but

God had wanted to heal Kay, He would have restored her health no matter what I did. If God had not wanted her to live, all our efforts would not have succeeded. It is not what I tell or ask God to do that attains the results I want. He is Lord, and my best course of action is to cooperate with what He says is best. He asks me to love Him, trust Him, and commune with Him so that I can understand Him better.

Jesus said of Himself that He came to His hour to glorify God the Father. Over the past years, thousands of people have heard and read Kay's story—and Christ has been glorified through it.

*For Discussion*

1. How would you explain a "resurrection" to a non-Christian?

2. Is it harder to believe in Christ's resurrection than in Kay Lynne's healing?

3. Why do many people deny the resurrection of Jesus Christ?

4. What difference does His resurrection make in your life?

5. In light of this story, how do you understand the saying, "Love the Lord for who He is, not for what He does"?

# CHAPTER 3

## Keri

*K*eri Mitchell lives in Fairfax, Virginia, where her father is pastor of a church. Before her sickness she was a healthy, happy child who learned quickly in school. Her parents, Dennis and Etta Mae, are devoted Christians who believe that their work with God is of eternal significance.

"I think your little girl has a brain tumor. I want her in the Charlottesville University Hospital today."

Although it took only a few minutes of consultation for the neurologist to make that diagnosis, Keri Mitchell's symptoms had actually started five months earlier. In May 1973, five-year-old Keri began vomiting in the morning. "My neck hurts," she often complained. The doctor who checked her could find nothing wrong. In July she demonstrated an unusually strong desire to stay near her mother. That clinging increased markedly in August.

One day in early September she fell while riding her bicycle. She found she couldn't get up and walk to the house. When Keri's mother Etta Mae saw her daughter's plight, she was frightened.

"There's something terribly wrong with Keri! We've got to have the doctor find out what it is!" she told her husband.

When a series of X-ray pictures revealed no abnormalities, the doctor referred Keri to a neurologist for brain tests. A brief examination revealed gross abnormalities in Keri's nervous system. "I'm sure these changes in Keri are caused by a brain tumor," the neurologist told the Mitchells.

Dennis, Keri's father, later described his reaction to that incredible news: "My first thought was: I'm a Christian; I'm trusting in God. I believe that God heals. I am obligated to express my faith. Do I rush her to a doctor or do I say, 'We believe in prayer,' then wait and pray? I thought about it awhile; then I had the distinct feeling that it was my responsibility to do all I could, medically, while waiting on God. I concluded that this was not a denial of faith."

Another pastor lived nearby, a man whose prayers for the sick often seemed effective. When Dennis returned home he called that pastor. "We've made arrangements to take Keri down to the University Hospital in Charlottesville," Dennis said. "I am asking God to touch her body, but I plan to have the doctors do whatever needs to be done for her as long as God doesn't intervene to heal her miraculously. What would you do, Pastor?"

The pastor replied, "Dennis, I would do exactly as you're doing."

That afternoon Dennis called his church secretary. "Please take the calls and explain the problem," he said, "and ask the people please not to call me. I don't want to be rude or inconsiderate. I just don't want to talk to people over and over again about it right now."

In Charlottesville, Dennis found that the doctors and nurses who were to attend Keri were marvelous: "They gave us the impression that there was no other child in University Hospital but Keri." They kept the family well informed. Keri had more tests and interviews that first afternoon than would normally be given in the course of several days. Later in the evening, since no room was yet available for Etta Mae at the hospital, the Mitchells asked to take Keri with them to a nearby motel. The doctors, however, said they wanted to watch her all night.

## Surgery

That period in the lives of the Mitchell family produced many anxious moments. In a letter to those concerned about their family, they wrote:

Dear Friends,

Thank you, thank you, thank you for your prayers and expressions of concern for Keri. We have depended on you so much, and you have helped us reach out to God.

On September 11, the tests and examinations began at the hospital. The doctors were so concerned about the pressure on Keri's eyes that the operating room was alerted for a possible emergency operation. The next day a four-vessel cerebral shunt was installed from the brain to the abdomen to relieve the pressure on Keri's brain.

The planned operation to remove the tumor from her brain was delayed because of the slow and difficult recovery from the shunt operation. The doctors said they had never had a child at that hospital with so much pressure on her eyes.

On September 24 at 10 A.M., the tests on the brain were complete, and the brain tumor was located in the cerebellum. By 12:30 P.M. Keri was in the operating room.

At 5:30, the surgeon said, "Surgery is finished. We found a benign brain tumor, longer and larger than a hen's egg. It is a low-grade tumor, the kind to have if you're going to have a tumor. I had to make a choice, because I had to try to get out all of the tumor I possibly could so it would not return. But in trying, I may have hurt Keri. The part of her brain on which I worked controls breathing and swallowing, and we will know within three hours if she can breathe and swallow. If so, you still have to wait two weeks, during which time her life will hang in the balance."

At that point I suppose we should have felt the most anxiety of that whole time. But strangely enough we experienced a time of calmness and trust. We bowed our heads together while a man from our church led us in prayer. "Thank you, God, for taking care of Keri," he prayed simply.

In less than three hours the doctors returned with good news: "It's really encouraging. You have every reason to be happy." Keri could breathe.

We were very excited and grateful. But the doctors again warned us that it would be at least two weeks before the outcome would be known for certain. Those two weeks proved to be only the beginning of another ordeal, which included four more operations.

On September 30, an infection began in Keri's head. The medication given for it sometimes causes harmful side effects, but it had to be administered for at least a week.

> Your friends,
> Dennis and Etta Mae Mitchell

Keri received as many as thirty-nine shots a week, including spinal taps. Would it be possible for her to survive? The Mitchells kept waiting for God to intervene.

In mid-October the doctors postponed an operation several times because of infection and fever. At the same time they continued to express concern that the antibiotic required to control the infection might cause deafness. Finally, at the end of October, Keri went to the operating room. She returned with her new shunt, which the surgeon made long enough that it might never need to be lengthened. That shunt made possible the beginning of real recovery. The Mitchells thanked God for success.

Throughout that time Dennis and Etta Mae drew strength from the prayers, cards, phone calls, and letters that came not only from their own congregation but from people all over the United States. Expressions of love arrived in many different forms from people in similar situations. "We have never been more thankful for God's people or overwhelmed by their outpouring of compassion," Dennis said. "We praise God for His wonderful love and pray that we and Keri will be able to serve Him effectively."

Dennis drove one hundred miles each way to visit his daughter. On one of those trips he had an experience he could not have anticipated.

"As I drove all that way I had time for a lot of thinking and praying. I shed a lot of tears between Fairfax and Charlottesville. I just couldn't understand how God would let this happen.

"By this time people all over the United States were agreeing frequently in prayer for Keri's healing. With all the promises in the Bible, obviously a lot of people would lose faith in God if Keri did not experience physical healing. Why would God stand by and let such a thing happen? Then, somehow, I came to realize that I didn't have to worry about God's reputation. He would take care of that. I felt deep down inside that God would take care of me and that He would take care of Keri and our whole family in His own way—not necessarily in mine."

During that ordeal the people of Pastor Mitchell's congregation demonstrated understanding and grace. One particular Wednesday evening Dennis conducted a business meeting at the church. Following the meeting he asked the congregation to remain because he had a request to make of them. He explained that his wife felt sure that Keri would be healed, but he needed their prayers and support. His own faith seemed to be slipping. The people gathered in the front of the church at the altar and along the front row to pray for their pastor.

The Mitchells leaned heavily on Arlo Newell, another pastor whose son had required a shunt from his brain as well as six major operations to correct a malfunction in his body. Because Arlo Newell could say, "I've been where you are, I care for you, and I love you," the Mitchells received strength and encouragement.

As Dennis says, "Many times before, I had felt compassion for people who had problems. But I had wondered what I could do other than say, 'Look, I'm sorry for you.' So I went on my way, feeling bad for the person, praying, but not really being able to express my deep concern. Now I have learned how much it means to say, 'I care, I really care. I'm praying for you.'"

Several times during the uncertainty, Etta Mae and Dennis felt it would be much easier to accept Keri's death than a permanent lifetime handicap. One morning Etta Mae called from the hospital to tell him that Keri was apparently blind. "That was one of my hardest moments," Dennis recalls.

God accomplished much healing in their lives during those weeks. They were especially thankful for the new understanding and sense of compassion that He had given them. They did not know what the future might hold for Keri, what her improvement would be, or how she would be able to cope with life. On the other hand, they couldn't know what was ahead for themselves, either. That helped them realize they should be putting their best into life at every moment.

Keri came home on her sixth birthday, two months after she had entered the hospital. Her parents reported: "When we stopped in the yard, our cat ran out to the car, and Keri reached for him. She smiled for the first time since the operation and made a sound. We all cried for joy." Yet Keri did not walk or talk except to say "Mama." She cried, seemed fairly alert, and heard well. One major question remained. Her vision was impaired; would the loss of sight be permanent?

Two weeks went by. Then one day Keri spoke. "Mom, why can't I talk?" Her speech had returned! Soon her family had another shock. Keri began to express bitterness and anger. She was belligerent and nasty. After living with that for a few days, Dennis called the neurologist. "Keri will just have to learn to wait for things," the doctor replied. She would have to relearn, for example, that it takes time to cook a hamburger. The neurologist warned them that retraining and relearning would take a long time.

For a few days Keri's bitterness continued. Dennis left to attend an out-of-town evangelism clinic. One evening when he called home Keri wanted to talk to him. She wanted to sing him a song, which she did. She sang another, and another, until she had sung five songs.

When Dennis came home, he found Keri sitting in the living room in a chair. As he came through the door, she jumped out of the chair. "Daddy!" She had forgotten she couldn't walk! Dennis caught her.

Dennis describes Keri's change in personality the next two or three days as dramatic and pronounced. That didn't mean that her personality problem completely disappeared. Her nerves wore out before her energy did, yet she refused to rest at such times. She was demanding, and her parents sometimes found it difficult to be patient. They tried to help her understand that she needed to be flexible, that living with others always requires some give and take.

Keri continued to stumble. No one knew how much of her difficulty derived from the inability to see and how much was caused by the removal of a large portion of the cerebellum of her brain. Once when her parents took her back to the surgeon for a checkup, he remarked to several other doctors, "Look! See that child walk? I took out most of her cerebellum, but look at her go!" He was thrilled at the sight, and the onlookers were thrilled too.

Unquestionably, God's healing power let Keri come through her surgery much better than anyone had expected. Keri could walk, and her intelligence remained completely unaffected. Because her right eye was blind, she saw poorly, but at least she could see. Although her cerebral shunt continued as a permanent part of her anatomy, it functioned well. The surgeon said that if by some chance he had not removed all of the tumor, it probably would come back by the time she was thirteen years old. Meanwhile, he said, the Mitchells should live as though the tumor would not return.

By Christmas Keri was talking, laughing, and walking—unsteadily but independently. She wrapped presents for many people. During the church Christmas program she gave a recitation. The people laughed, clapped, and cried as they saw God's remarkable healing progress in action. Because her left arm and leg remained weak, her parents gave her a big-wheel tricycle for Christmas to exercise her legs. As she rode up and down the sidewalk all her friends watched her, happy that she could ride and play again.

Four months after Keri's brain surgery she sang a song for the doctor that she had often sung before the operation. Her singing surprised him, and her high mental level delighted him. Today, only when she asks for items already beside her does she betray the blindness in her right eye.

## A Mother's Response

Asked about her thoughts on healing throughout Keri's illness, Etta Mae Mitchell paused thoughtfully before she replied. "I don't know anything to say in great philosophical or theological terms. Simply, I feel the Lord was so good to Keri and our family. It sometimes seems as if we haven't gone through much, yet when we talk to the doctors I realize Keri has gone through a lot and could very well be blind and deaf now or might not have survived at all.

"I always hoped she would be instantly healed and no operations would be necessary. We hoped that the tumor would simply go away without surgery. Now I see that the Lord worked for us to find a top-notch neurologist who sent us to a good hospital and good surgeons. The Lord has allowed Keri to see and hear and still have good mental capacity, even after all the antibiotics and operations she's had.

"At one point I questioned if something in my life was preventing the Lord from answering my prayers for Keri's immediate healing. My faith was strengthened by sharing with a Christian doctor who helped me to see that this was not the case. When I could say, 'Lord, Thy will be done,' I felt peace. It was up to Him then whether she lived or died.

"The suffering Keri experienced was the hardest to bear. I gained a new perspective on the need for patience. I see that life can go on at church without my doing so much.

"Keri put it well when she said, 'Mom, I have so many

more friends now because I was sick.' Our outlook on life has broadened. I met a woman who lost a child and now sends me questions about life after death. I correspond with some of the nurses. Through Keri's illness God has opened up new avenues of service and witnessing for all of us."

Two and a half years after Keri went home from the hospital another letter came from the Mitchells:

Dear Friends,
   Keri is now in the third grade and doing excellent work. She turned eight in November. Her blind eye and shunt don't seem to limit her activities. She especially enjoys the monkey bars in physical education class and climbing trees at home.
   The doctors still refer to her as "unbelievable" and a "miracle." We accept her daily as a gift from God and remember the horrors only as we tell what she came through. We do not understand divine healing, nor do we know why God dealt so kindly with us. We told our congregation that we do not have nearly so many answers as we used to have, but we have much more faith.
   Perhaps we have been able to help others as we acknowledge the spiritual struggle that this kind of experience brings. We thank God for the spiritual victory also.

Your friends,<br>
Dennis and Etta Mae Mitchell

*The Refining of Faith*
*Read 1 Peter 1:3–9.*
   Dennis Mitchell's first reaction to the tragic news of his daughter's brain tumor triggered a flurry of emotion. "Why me? I'm a Christian!" Many Christians ask that question

when sickness strikes, as though we think we should be exempted from suffering.

As I studied Keri's case and talked with the Mitchells, I became aware that the 1 Peter 1:3–9 passage reveals an attitude toward suffering that Christians do not always apply. We do not usually rejoice; we do not immediately see such experiences as opportunities for our faith to shine through.

Our grief and the immensity of the immediate problem obscure the view that all that happens is God-filtered. It is hard to grasp the concept that a loving God is in control when someone we love is in such pain.

*For Discussion*

1. When you hear of a small child critically injured in an auto accident or ill with a devastating disease, how do you react? How do you reconcile seemingly useless suffering with God's love? How can we lean on God and give over everything to Him and still respond to human need as compassionate human beings?

2. If you were in a situation similar to the Mitchells', what do you think you would be able to share out of your reservoir of faith?

3. Dennis and Etta Mae have said that after this long ordeal they do not have nearly so many answers, but they have much more faith. What does this tell us about the nature of faith? Define faith; then try to imagine situations that would stretch your faith.

# CHAPTER 4
## Keith

*K*eith Grubbs, now a teen-ager, is the son of Jan and Jerry Grubbs. Jerry, who teaches religious education in seminary, had been a pastor for several years before accepting his present teaching assignment. Jan is secretary to the principal in an elementary school. Members of their congregation, as well as friends and students, attest to their deep love for God and His presence in their lives.

"What do you say when your nine-year-old son announces, 'When I go to the bathroom, it's all red'? If you're a mother, you play it cool, because that's the style of a mother. If you're a father, you go all to pieces." Their son Keith's announcement initiated a series of events that profoundly influenced the lives of the Grubbs family—parents, son, and daughter Kim.

The next morning Jerry and Jan took Keith to a favorite friend, their family doctor Bill Anderson. After an examination, Dr. Anderson immediately sent Keith to St. John's Hospital for X-rays. By mid-morning doctors were scurrying and conferring with each other.

"The first report that came to us went something like this: 'Your son might have cancer.' We heard neither the 'might' nor any of the other explanations. We heard only the red-flag word, *cancer*," Jerry explained.

The following Tuesday Keith was given crucial tests by a urologist. "I've never seen anything like this before," the urologist admitted.

A football injury to Keith the Wednesday before had opened the door to what would prove later to be a necessary healing process. Jerry remarked, "I'm sure God had his hand in this from the very beginning, including the injury and all that later occurred."

The doctors suspected and then confirmed that Keith had inherited a congenital kidney problem. Keith is one of those unusual persons who have more than two kidneys. The tumorlike third kidney, as the urologist described it, had grown and ballooned out of control. At the time of Keith's football injury, the abnormal kidney had destroyed half of his left kidney, fused itself to the bladder, and caused considerable damage to the internal organs.

A week later Keith underwent an operation to remove the growth from the kidney and bladder. The surgeon explained carefully to him what had happened and what to expect during the postoperative period. "We did not know as Tuesday began that it would be one of the longest days of our lives," Jerry and Jan recalled.

"I can never express in words the deep respect we have for Bill Anderson," Jerry said. "He's not only a wonderful doctor, he's a Christian doctor. Bill came in the evening before the operation. He told us that the surgeon was one of the best in that particular field. Then Bill said, 'Why don't we just pray about the operation?' There my family physician became my pastor. We knelt on the floor, with all the traffic of the pediatric ward going on around us, while he administered spiritual medicine that we greatly needed. That prayer touched not only my heart but Keith's too. I think it provided healing for him."

### Long Operation

"Another very important time for us occurred just before Keith was taken to the operating room. In prayer, Jan, Keith, and I placed Keith in God's hands, knowing that God could take care of him in the anticipated three-hour operation."

The three hours passed. Then a nurse came into the room where we were waiting. "It's going to be a little longer than we thought," she said calmly. Another hour passed. Finally Jerry walked out into the hallway where he found the urologist, the assisting doctor, and Dr. Anderson conferring with each other. "Well, how did it go?" Jerry asked.

"It was a good stopping point," they replied, "so we thought we'd take a break."

Needless to say, that remark filled the parents with anxiety. The operation had already gone an hour beyond the schedule, and the doctors were talking about a "break."

"We knew God could take care of a three-hour operation," Jerry mused, "but now we were beginning to wonder."

As time passed, the surgeon came out again and explained that the problem entailed much more than he had imagined from his examination of the X-ray pictures. For several hours the Grubbs waited, struggling to maintain their faith. During that time the surgeon removed half of the left kidney, disconnected the ureter from the bladder, and fused it to the bladder again.

Finally, after the seven-hour operation, Jerry and Jan visited their son. "I've been in hospitals as a pastor for a number of years," Jerry said. "I've seen many patients, but it was a very difficult experience to see my son lying there."

Yet Keith rebounded quickly. "We did not need to fret and worry and struggle. God had made that little body so that it could re-create itself, and it began to do just that."

The doctor, too, indicated his surprise at the rapid healing. Within a week the only signs of the operation were a bit of weakness, considerable weight loss, and the appearance of what Keith and Jerry lovingly refer to as the "little zipper" and the "big zipper." The surgeon had found it necessary to make a second major incision in order to correct the problem.

Keith left the hospital wearing a surgically implanted drainage system—bag and tube. The urologist had suggested that Keith would probably have to carry that equipment for one year while the kidney completely healed. After Keith's discharge from the hospital on the first of November, he recuperated at home for the rest of the month. His return to school had been planned for sometime after Thanksgiving. That seemed impossible, however.

"The maintenance of the drainage system caused many problems for Keith, Jan, and me. We had the constant ordeal of changing the padding, emptying the bag, and replacing the system with new bags," Jerry commented.

Thanksgiving Day was marked by a high moment for the family. "We were sharing Thanksgiving dinner with several families in our friendship circle," Jerry recalled. "Just before dinner, Keith sat down on my lap to catch his breath from having played very hard. I automatically reached over to check the drainage system and discovered that the bag was totally empty. I asked if he had just emptied it. 'No, Daddy,' he said, 'I haven't emptied it since last night.' Knowing how quickly the bag usually filled, I immediately realized that a problem might have developed with the system. Keith could be poisoning himself internally, as the urologist had warned us might happen.

"We immediately rushed Keith to the emergency room at St. John's Hospital. The doctor examined Keith and verified that the drainage had stopped. He preferred waiting until the next day, however, when all the hospital services would be available and the urologist would be back in town, to run a total check on Keith. I looked down at Keith and explained to him that the drainage had stopped, that there was some kind of difficulty, and that we would have to come back to the hospital tomorrow. Keith took my arm. 'Well, Daddy,' he said, 'isn't this what we've been praying for all this time?'

"The following day the X-ray pictures showed that the healing process had suddenly become complete. Keith did not need the external drainage system any longer. A great relief came over us. We rejoiced and thanked God for this miraculous healing."

Supporting the Grubbs throughout Keith's illness were friends, members of their church, and hospital personnel. "God worked through the pastoral staff of our church. Our family owes a great deal of gratitude to them. They came to talk and pray with us or to spend time with Keith. I remember Pastor Keith Huttenlocker's saying to him, 'We Keiths have to stick together.' I recall the many hours that Pastor David Coolidge spent with Jan and me. We needed his comforting arm and loving heart.

"And we appreciate the doctors and the St. John's Hospital staff. I've never known a group of persons who worked so harmoniously and lovingly together. They really did a splendid job of caring for Keith. The chaplain spent much time with us and became a close friend during that experience. And I especially appreciate the Sister who spotted Jan crying. The Sister found a private room and put her to bed for rest. 'This one is on us,' she said."

Keith wallpapered his hospital room with cards from friends all over the country. People the Grubbs knew, people they didn't know, people who had been friends years ago, sent their regards and assurances that they were praying.

"Mom, it seems like the whole world is praying for me," Keith said.

### Monument to a Miracle

Jerry continued, "Really, around the physical wholeness of Keith there developed a relational wholeness for our family. We were brought together with each other, with God, and with a whole community of Christian believers. I relearned for myself what it means to trust God. As a family, we discovered what Keith means to us.

"As far as we, as a family, are concerned, Keith is a monument to a miracle. His illness initially looked like an invader bent on destroying everything that we felt constituted our lives. We realize now that in the midst of Keith's disease God created new life for us. I don't know what tomorrow will bring, but today I'm thanking God. The miracle He worked in our family has given us a new awareness of His love, His people, and our love for each other. We have a constant awareness that God is real."

### Coping With Illness
### Read Romans 8:26–28.

Several things in this portion of Scripture can help us cope with illness. (1) The Spirit of God comes to our aid in our weakness. (2) When we need Him the most, He is there to intercede for us. (3) Even when we are inarticulate, the Spirit of God Himself presents our case to God. It is a consolation to know that, no matter how difficult a situation may be we still have access to God the Father. He knows our deepest and innermost longings. (4) These verses assure us that God cooperates for good in all the things that happen to us.

If God is for us, it doesn't matter who is against us. The apostle Paul tells us that God did not spare even His own Son but gave Him up for all of us. We can have great confidence in God, therefore, that He will spare nothing in our behalf so that we might become the full, mature beings that He designed and created us to be. We can accept any of our problems as opportunities to grow, develop, and mature.

The final verses of this passage, Romans 8:35-39, emphasize that nothing can separate us from the love of God.

**For Discussion**

1. Jan and Jerry saw Keith as a living miracle. Spend a few minutes considering just what was miraculous about his healing.

2. Would Keith's healing be more miraculous if it had been an instantaneous healing?

3. How did this healing include more than just Keith?

4. Describe ways in which you can share in God's healing ministry when you are caring for a sick person. What Bible verses have helped you face difficult situations?

5. Talk to someone in the next week and explain to that person what you believe a miracle is. Describe what miracles have occurred in your own life or in the lives of people you know personally.

# CHAPTER 5
# Lawrence

*The Reverend Lawrence Brooks was a retired minister. He loved to write songs and poems taken from specific experiences in his life. As an active layman in his local church, he contributed much to people's lives.*

"I am here in Community Hospital awaiting an operation at 1 P.M. tomorrow," Lawrence Brooks explained. "I'm to have a section of my colon removed."

He had come to the hospital five days earlier for tests and X-rays. Through this time of waiting he had kept busy reading and writing. Unable to attend church Sunday, he had written two poems. One was a hymn of praise that began, "Sing of God's power sent down from above. . . ." The other spoke of the peace he had found in Jesus Christ, a peace still "flowing like a river" on the eve of major surgery.

Lawrence thought seriously about his situation. "At age eighty-one and with the variety of problems I've faced during these years, I have very little trouble relaxing in the face of whatever comes. Worry complicates matters and hinders faith. Likewise, I give little time to fretting about my problems. So much more joy and satisfaction come from constructive thinking or working.

"Worry wastes my time. I cannot change my situation, so worry is a sign that my faith in God is not operative. For a long time now I have refused to worry about things I don't understand or can't help. It is wonderful to be able to trust my present situation entirely to God and the surgeon. In doing so I can turn my attention to other matters. Now I am on the lookout for chances to witness for my Lord. They always come."

Since Lawrence Brooks completely trusted his present and future to God and His direction, he experienced what he described as "the wonderful undisturbed joy of living." He believed confidently that each day would be a better day. One of his favorite Bible verses was "The path of the just is as the shining light, that shineth more and more unto the perfect day" (Prov. 4:18 KJV). Consequently, as Lawrence prepared for surgery he could say, "My joy and happiness in the service of my Master are richer and fuller as the days pass. I have absolutely no fear of what may happen."

On the day of the operation Lawrence's fifteen-year-old roommate also underwent surgery. The following day the boy awoke by 9 A.M. Lawrence was still quite groggy. He recalled lying in bed with his "nervous system all shot."

"I just wanted people to leave me alone. I felt 'harnessed up' to a stomach pump and intravenous feedings, as well as to other tubes and straps."

Within a few minutes his roommate turned on the television. "An hour or two later I was fed up with teen-age programs," Lawrence recalled. "But I might as well not have been, because they didn't end until eleven o'clock that night. Anyone who has gone through a major operation knows how I felt the first day after surgery. All those television programs were pretty hard to take. I was tempted to feel sorry for myself.

"Finally a nurse came in. I asked her, 'Is there anything you could do to control the television?' I had the bed next to the window, and the television was placed so that it was directly in front of me. I couldn't get away from it.

" 'No,' she said frankly but kindly. 'He paid for it, so it's his. As long as he pays the rental fee he can use it anytime he wants, day or night.'

"That was a hard blow. Suddenly a couple of Scripture passages came to my mind. One tells of Christ's forty days in the wilderness and His temptation (see Matt. 4:1-11). Another passage tells us that Jesus was tempted at all points as we are (see Heb. 4:15). He didn't have television in His day, but He had something worse—the Pharisees. At least I didn't have them.

"I began praying and thinking things over. I acknowledged to myself, 'Yes, that boy paid for this television. He can use it when he wants to, so you shouldn't try to control him. You can take it. It isn't as bad as you think.' "

Then Lawrence remembered the special friendship the two of them had begun before their operations. "Was I going to spoil all that with my present selfishness? True, I was in pain, weak, and nervous. But you know, after I decided to endure the situation, it wasn't half as bad as it was before. If a person can get his head straightened out, and his heart, he doesn't need much else. Later I had other, similar temptations, but with God's help I found victory over all of them. So God helped me save my witness with that boy."

*Lessons*

"I found out one thing a little better than I had known it before. I could learn to laugh at my problems, smile at my temptation, and save my witness. I could have gotten all stirred up and maybe said a lot of things that weren't very Christian. I could have pulled all kinds of alibis for acting selfishly, but there's really no excuse for doing so. Jesus had grace, and He wants to share it with us so we can exhibit it for Him. He'll help us through any problem that comes, whether we're well and robust or flat on our back."

Finally the day came for Lawrence's young friend to leave. The young man, with his father and mother, bid Lawrence a joyous and friendly goodbye. After their departure Lawrence began to look forward to a good night's rest. That anticipation was a bit premature. God had something else in mind, as Lawrence soon found out. That afternoon the aides wheeled in a sixty-year-old man with painful muscle spasms.

"If you've ever had muscle spasms," Lawrence said, "you know what suffering is. I've had a few that didn't last very long, but his were continuous. Immediately I saw that my night's rest was shot, so I started praying for my roommate. Generally I try to go to sleep around 9 P.M. That night I said to the Lord, 'Tonight is Yours. Whatever You want me to do, You help me to understand and do it.' After midnight the nurses finally were able to quiet him. Then I was able to sleep."

The next morning the nurses woke Lawrence at 6 A.M. Although he hadn't had a full night's sleep, he felt prepared to share his faith with his new roommate. A minister friend visited Lawrence later that morning, and they were able to talk and have prayer with the other patient. "So I had a wonderful time of fellowship with this gentleman during the next few days," he recalled.

Lawrence had many opportunities to witness to people easily and naturally. "Now that my surgery is history," he said eight days after surgery, "I have something more to say. My faith in God and my surgeon have been completely confirmed. The section of my colon they removed, according to all reports, was malignant. And all the affected parts were removed. My doctor says I have made satisfactory improvement.

"It seems possible now that I may have more time for serving the Lord. I value very much any time I have left, and I deeply desire the best use of however many days are still allotted to me. My stay at the hospital was wonderful, filled with many interesting experiences. As God and I dealt with those experiences, I discovered value in them that I shall never forget. For instance, I had a challenging course in patience and self-control—virtues I normally find hard to practice.

"I have a strong conviction that God permitted that experience because He couldn't teach me some things without it. That brief illness may mean a redirection of many of my activities and a more meaningful use of my time. My stay in the hospital resulted in as much good for me spiritually as any other way.

"I'm still milking those experiences for all I can get out of them. What's the use of having to go through the same course twice? I'm determined not to do it. I think I'm better prepared to live out the rest of my days. The thing I'm most happy about is that He taught me how to save my witness!"

Lawrence Brooks's experience demonstrates that we can count on the presence of God in our trials when we trust Him. Why did he feel so strongly that God helped him to "save his witness"? If you had asked him about his witness for Christ, he would have taken you back to the time in his life when he became a Christian and determined to become a minister. Back in 1934 he wrote a hymn about the contrast in his life before and after he trusted Christ. That hymn, "He Lifted Me Out," was a statement of Christ's power to save and redirect a life. It was that witness that Lawrence Brooks did not want to go back on, forty years later.

*Our Call to Positive Witness*
*Read Luke 12:8–12.*

Lawrence Brooks's major concern was his desire to tell others what God had done for him. Often people find it difficult to talk to others about their relationship with God, particularly when they themselves are sick.

For many of us, illness is such a trying experience that we are unable to spend much time witnessing about Christ. Lawrence's life gives us a fundamental perspective on coping with life that can help us rise above the destructive effect of physical illness. Luke 12:8–12 gives us a better understanding of Lawrence's concerns.

We see from this passage that Christ calls us to share our witness with others. We are to acknowledge Him before all persons, regardless of our circumstances. As Lawrence speaks with individuals, he does not consider his own situation but the people to whom he can relate the message of Jesus Christ. As he learns about them and their needs, and expresses his dependence on God, he finds that God's Holy Spirit gives him perceptive understanding. When others see what God has done in his life, the positive witness is undeniable.

Lawrence chose his priorities wisely. His songs and his testimony show that God is faithful. Lawrence's witness is ongoing.

*For Discussion*

1. What is your witness? Think back to a frightening or tragic circumstance in your past. Ask yourself, "What did I

portray to others as the essence of my own philosophy and theology through that experience?"

2. What type of person was I before I met Jesus Christ? Have I been able to witness victory over the "old me"? Have I continued developing the "new me" through Christ? Read and ponder Colossians 3:8–15.

3. What Scripture passages are meaningful to you as you share your witness with others?

4. If you were to write a book about your life, what would be its central theme? If you were to produce a play in which you were the central figure, how would you show your audience what God has done in your life?

# CHAPTER 6
## Paul

*B*arbara Clausen and her husband Paul served as associate ministers for a number of years before pastoring their first congregation. Paul was an especially good singer and choir director. Since Paul's devastating illness, Barbara has worked full time as secretary and as mother in order to raise their two children, now in college. She has donated hundreds of hours and dollars to help educate people about Huntington's disease. In 1975 Barbara testified before a new federal commission on Huntington's disease. Barbara tells their story.

"You will spend the next fifteen to twenty years in slow deterioration and end up in a hospital bed with none of your normal bodily functions. If you are more fortunate, you will die of a heart attack or pneumonia at an early age."

Those words were spoken by doctors at the Mayo Clinic to Paul Clausen, my husband. It's not easy to be given such a prognosis at thirty-five years of age.

Paul had been examined and tested for two days, and his family history reviewed. Then the doctors confirmed the diagnosis of Huntington's disease. "Go home and live with it," they said. "We have no control drug, no cure."

That afternoon and evening we spent the most difficult hours of our lives in a motel room in Rochester, Minnesota. Another cruel blow hit us as we pondered the future—we would eventually have to tell our two children the facts about the disease and the fifty-fifty chance that they would inherit it.

Paul enjoyed life. He loved to sing, preach, and be with young people. How would he handle such devastating news? At first he tried to accept the verdict—the "sentence," as he called it—for a crime he did not commit.

*Early Symptoms*

Our story goes back about eleven years. We did not need a tragedy to bring our family to the Lord. We had served Him to the best of our abilities for many years. We were pastoring our first congregation after many years of associate pastoral work. We enjoyed our two small children, loved our work, and felt very secure. Yet stealthily and cunningly, strange symptoms—fear, fatigue, depression, change in personality, loss of interest in work and in our family—began to occur in my husband. Those symptoms appeared and disappeared in ominous cycles for about eighteen months.

During that time we visited local doctors. The diagnoses varied: Paul needed vitamin B-1 shots; was just overtired; was under too much stress; must learn to relax; was in the wrong kind of work. We visited more clinics and hospitals, and finally Paul resigned from our church. We moved to another city for a different environment, and he took a part-time job. The symptoms increased. At last we decided that a trip to the Mayo Clinic would provide a thorough checkup and consultation. My husband knew of a history of Huntington's chorea in his family, since his mother had died of it. But he disliked talking about it—a common characteristic of those having the disease.

Huntington's disease is one of two thousand known genetic diseases, a neurological dysfunction like Parkinson's disease, multiple sclerosis, and epilepsy. Usually the patient's family history tells the story; the children have a fifty-fifty chance of inheriting the disease. Identified by Dr. George Huntington over a hundred years ago, the disease began as a genetic mutation and was brought to this country from England in the early 1600s. Until 1967, the few facts and statistics available to the medical profession had permitted only one thousand positive diagnoses of the disease. Since the organization in 1967 of the Committee to Combat Huntington's Disease, 100,000 cases have been identified. This extremely severe disease causes a progressive mental and physical deterioration for fifteen to twenty years and eventually results in complete loss of bodily functions. One by one the good things of life are taken away. It is a hard and cruel death.

Depression and anxiety severely blighted Paul. I watched him go through stages of denial, anger, bargaining. Necessity demanded, finally, that he enter a psychiatric hospital. We both knew then that the end had begun. The bottom had dropped out of life.

Despite thousands of prayers for his healing being offered, healing didn't happen. We believed and prayed for a miracle. We attended church services where many pastors anointed and prayed for Paul while the whole church joined in praying for his healing. Letters and cards came from across the country, from around the world, giving us courage. We prayed and waited. It seemed that God had deserted us when we needed Him most. Had He?

I remember walking into our son's bedroom one afternoon to look at the picture of Jesus hanging on the wall. Jesus' arms were outstretched. Through tears I told Him that things were falling apart. He had let us down completely. I couldn't believe that He loved us or cared for us at all. In utter despair I started to leave the room when I heard the words, *Where are you going?*

I stopped and sat on the bed, thoughts flooding my mind. Where *would* I go? What would I do? Our lives had been centered around the church. I looked up at that picture again, and those outstretched arms seemed to be outstretched for *me*. I decided at that moment to trust Him. I knew that my life with its problems would be better with God than without Him.

That decision proved right. God has sustained me and my family more than I believed possible. We've had many problems that seemed to overwhelm us. Most of the time it has required sheer will power and determination to hang on.

**The Multiplication Factor**

I wish I could tell you that after my experience of recommitment things began to go easier and we were able to cope with life a little better. Actually, our problems began to multiply. I had become the family breadwinner, but my salary was inadequate for the many household bills, medical and hospital bills, and unexpected expenses that always seemed to arise.

The events of the next two years seem unreal now, but they happened. Even though we had a major tragedy in our family, we weren't shielded from other problems. It was as if Satan had decided to launch a full-fledged attack designed to destroy not only my husband but me too.

When we moved from our mobile home into a house we lost money on the sale, just when we needed appliances and furniture. Not long after people from the church came and painted the rooms for us, we noticed soot and dusty cobwebs hanging on the pictures and draperies and walls. The fire chief finally came and found a faulty chimney; everything had to be cleaned, washed, or discarded.

When my sister tried to surprise us at Christmastime by putting decorations on our tree, she laid the tree lights out on the living room carpet to test them; every light burned a black hole in the carpet. When men from the church put up paneling in the bathroom, they laid it out in the kitchen to put glue on the back: the pilot light on the gas stove caused the flammable glue to explode, destroying a chair, curtains, part of the floor, and the cupboards.

The furnace failed in the middle of winter, and we had to get a new motor. In late spring a blizzard blew the television antenna away, along with part of the roof. During a terrible wind and rain storm, I went off the highway at the proper exit but ended up in a viaduct full of water that flooded the car. My son and I had to scramble out quickly.

The following summer our daughter Karen contracted mononucleosis. Shortly after her illness, she and I both had to undergo extensive tests for allergies. Those were just a few of the crises our family faced.

Through all our struggles my deepest and most sincere prayers centered on Paul. I prayed that he would be able to accept his illness and live with it, and that our children and I might be able to love him, care for him, and help him face his altered life. After one particularly bad weekend at the hospital, I drove home feeling discouraged and defeated. I didn't sleep well that night. Frequently I prayed something like this: "Oh, God, let me be able to help him. He has no one else. Let me be able to help him."

A couple of days later I drove to the hospital again, not expecting much of a reception. To my amazement Paul came smiling to greet me. His face appeared relaxed and almost radiant. I knew that something wonderful had happened. Although he had difficulty putting his experience into words, he shared as much of it as he could: He had been sitting alone on a bench in the hospital yard feeling rejected, bitter, and hostile toward everyone. He felt someone sit down at the other end of the bench and looked to see who it was. No one was there, yet he felt a warm presence that moved toward him until it seemed to envelop him completely.

"I felt God again," Paul told me. "I know He's going to be with me. I know He loves me because of you."

I reported the change in him to the doctors. They told me he would slip back into the stages of depression and that many of his former problems would arise from time to time. But let me tell you, their prediction never came true. The children and I enjoy a relationship with Paul that never ceases to amaze us. I must emphasize that the nature of the disease usually causes family tensions and conflicts which are almost never resolved. Many marriages end in divorce or shattered relationships. Our family teetered on the edge of that precipice before Paul had his encounter with God.

In 1970 we transferred Paul to a general hospital only twelve miles from home. We saw him several times a week and brought him home for visits. Everything went well for about eight months, until we found that our major medical insurance was being terminated. Since our medical bills amounted to seven hundred dollars a month, I could not afford his care without insurance.

After exhausting all avenues of help offered to me except divorce—which would make Paul a dependent of the state—I decided that he should return to the state hospital. Although the decision was very difficult for me, Paul accepted it with great poise and the assurance that everything would work out all right. He now lives in the chronic medical section of the Kalamazoo State Hospital.

### *Trusting*

I cannot assure any individual of divine healing. Dedicated Christians suffer and die every day. Accidents destroy or maim some. Others remain crippled or blind. Christians are not exempt. The old cliché that illness or grief comes into our lives as a test or punishment is dangerous, because it makes a Christian feel as if he or she has done something wrong when healing does not come. Instead of repeating old clichés, I would rather talk about God's love and grace and the blessings we can continue to enjoy. As Eugenia Price said in her book *No Pat Answers* what you don't need when your heart is breaking or your mind is shrinking with fear is a challenge to greater spirituality.[1] What you need then is hope; hope that after some time has passed by God's grace and love you can begin to function again. We need to hear Jesus' statement again and again, "I will be with you always."

As I encounter suffering and grief, I find that I desperately need friends. We have many wonderful friends who keep in touch with us. Every Christmas brings beautiful cards, notes, and gifts, and I am always overwhelmed by that expression of love and loyalty. I've often wondered what would have happened to our family had it not been for our friends and the family of God.

Now let me get into what I call the nitty-gritty of the matter. It's not enough for someone just to say "I'll pray for you." Sometimes I need a handclasp that says "I care." Other times I need to be included in what others are doing. The changeover from one style of living to another brought about by separation from a loved one, whether by death or not, is indescribably difficult. I need understanding and patience, because the easiest thing to do in the midst of my grief is to retreat from those around me. What I don't need are the pat answers that are usually thrown my way: "This is God's will for you. God is teaching you a lesson. You'll just have to pray more. You'll have to have more faith."

Perhaps someone can tell me why an elderly man lives on in a nursing home and cannot die, when a young man wants to live and cannot get well. Or why a young girl is killed in a car accident and a Christian woman in her nineties wants to go to be with the Lord and cannot. Or why a longed-for baby is born dead or deformed. Or why a young mother or father is dying of cancer while her or his children need to be parented.

I don't know why millions of people are starving to death while our garbage cans overflow. Does God love them less? I don't know why a family is murdered while sleeping in their home, or why a young boy lies in a hospital like a vegetable as the result of a highway accident.

Paul and I have seen people in all those situations during the years of our ministry. We have watched good people, wonderful families suffer. Many of our friends have died from accidents, cancer, heart attacks, and other diseases. Two of our close friends were murdered.

Homes are wrecked by divorce, children are abused by the thousands, young people are destroyed by drugs and adults by alcohol. Every week at the Kalamazoo State Hospital I see the worst that life can deal. Those things happen in Christian homes, too. I don't understand it. It's part of a mystery that we can't understand.

But I know this. God loves all of His creation. He loves with a redemptive and everlasting love. I am certain of this: In the midst of tragedy or crisis I must find peace with God or I will perish. I am compelled to decide if God is a punishing, death-dealing God or if He has the same nature as our Lord Jesus Christ, who walked the earth healing, ministering, and, yes, even weeping.

In his book *O Susan*, James Angel wrote about his young daughter's death at age twenty in a car accident. "God comes to us in our crumbling moments. Not with theological rationale but with quiet affection. His promise is power and endurance to those who believe in and wait upon him."[2]

There is only one place where I can find rest for the anxieties of my heart. That place is in the childlike trust that God eventually gives us. If I can firmly believe in the love of God, I can make it.

Another person has said, "God is faith that comes when there is no reason for faith." Clearly, I had to determine my own image of God. I chose to see Him as a caring Jesus. I refuse to believe that Christ loves my family less than He loves yours or anyone else's because physical healing did not come to us.

*Helps to Wholeness*

Just as there are many hindrances to wholeness, there are also many helps. A modern, understandable translation of the Bible added dimension to my devotions. Good books that deal with the realities of life have been a tremendous source of help. They deal with situations I myself face.

I practice looking for sources of strength in nature, such as seeing a tulip bulb in the fall and imagining what it will look like in the spring. I believe in the Resurrection. As I think of the roots of trees that delve deep into the earth for strength and water, I remember God's strength. Underneath me remain His everlasting arms. I don't get nearly so tired when I remember that God sustains me.

The practice of stewardship has become more important. I

give God His fair share of my earnings, time, and service. Attending the worship services of my church fills my empty emotional life. Music in particular provides a great therapy.

My major problems center in loneliness and self-pity. Self-pity caused me to retreat from life, to find comfort only in solitude. Such a course of action proved unhealthy and unwise. Because I had always been a giver, I had to learn how to receive gratefully. I had to put forth the effort to live for my own and my children's sake, rather than for my husband's. Our children Karen and Dave express concern and compassion for their dad in their weekly trips to see him. They look for ways to show their love for him. I have been so thankful for their help and encouragement.

In my desperation to seek Paul's healing, I bought books, read articles, and watched televised mass-healing services. I was tempted to take him to such a service. But after much contemplation and soul-searching, I realized that Jesus' first concern is with individuals. He never prayed over a large crowd and hoped that some of them would be healed. Rather, he healed *each* person who came to him. My heart goes out to the thousands of persons who return home from healing services thinking that God loves them less than He loves others because they are still ill. Some studies have shown that many of those people leave the meeting worse off than before because of the physical letdown and mental depression that follow exposure to such services. Many refuse to take any more medication and die needlessly when doctors and good medication could have sustained them in useful living.

Contemporary Christianity often emphasizes external, spectacular occurrences. I believe the church's real ministry focuses on redeeming souls and teaching people how to cope with the situations in which they find themselves. The

Christian's life is not without problems, in spite of what some people say. The lives of Jesus, the apostles, and other Bible personalities were all filled with challenges and hardships. The words of Albert Schweitzer help me: "And to those who obey him, whether they be wise or simple, he will reveal himself in the toils, the conflict, the suffering which they shall pass through in his fellowship. And as an ineffable mystery they shall learn in their own experience who he is."[3]

James Angel's book says, "Faith at its deepest level is trust, hope is confidence, and love is redemptive."[4] I believe that with all my heart. What can separate us from the love of God? Can tragedy? Disease? Can anything really separate us from the love of God unless we allow it to? I believe God works *through our circumstances* as we live within His will. I cannot believe in Him or love Him or serve Him otherwise.

Discussing the apostle Paul, one person said it had been God's will that Paul be in jail so that he could write his great letters to the various churches. Another disagreed. "No, it was God's will that Paul write the letters, but it was the Roman ruler's will that he be in jail."

I like the second person's point of view. Jesus said that while we live in the world we will have tribulation, but that He has overcome the world (see John 16:33). Therefore, we have two possible responses to our suffering: We can become bitter, cynical, and of no use to ourselves or anyone else; or we can accept our circumstances and allow God to work through us and within us.

Recently I reread a Scripture passage that has often bothered me. Many times I've heard people say that we must give thanks *for* everything. I've never been able to be thankful for my husband's illness. I've never been thankful that my children have been deprived of their father and that we had so few years of life and work together.

But as I read that verse again I realized that it says "*In* every thing give thanks . . . " (1 Thess. 5:18 KJV, italics mine). That's quite different, isn't it? *Within* our circumstances we have found many reasons to be thankful. Strength comes when I think I cannot go another step. Help comes through encounters with people I have never known and in strange places: an elevator, a K-Mart garage, a hospital room. Burdens seem lighter when someone walks with me day by day and shares the yoke I bear. I know that redemptive love develops the trust and hope that carry me through each day.

I wish my husband might have been able to share this story with you and express those experiences of his which I will never know. I deeply admire Paul for his courage, trust, and ability to live through this debilitating illness, especially since both of his sisters have died of Huntington's disease during his illness.

When Paul could still talk we often prayed together, sang together, and talked about heaven. He assured me that he will sing again one day, and that he will occupy first chair in the baritone section of the heavenly choir—that is, if he doesn't get to direct the choir! I told him that many of our musically talented friends would be bidding for that job, but they're going to have terrible competition if he really wants it. I know Paul is at peace with God. He has no fear of death, and for that I am grateful.

A beautiful song came to our attention a few years ago. We did not get to sing it together, but we learned to love the words and it became our theme song. This song has been a continual source of strength to me.

> He giveth more grace when the burdens grow greater,
> He sendeth more strength when the labors increase;

To added affliction He addeth His mercy,
To multiplied trials, His multiplied peace.

When we have exhausted our store of endurance,
When our strength has failed ere the day is half done,
When we reach the end of our hoarded resources,
Our Father's full giving is only begun.

His love has no limit, His grace has no measure,
His power has no boundary known unto men;
For out of His infinite riches in Jesus,
He giveth, and giveth, and giveth again.[5]

### Demonstrating Faith
### Read James 1:2–5

Barbara Clausen is an example of faith and grace. As she encounters the major tragedy of her husband's Huntington's disease, she depends on the Lord for strength and endurance. The above verses in the book of James explain how our trials can help us mature and become strong.

Barbara Clausen reflects a basic attitude of steadfastness in asking God for the ability to meet each problem that arises. That kind of endurance results from seeing all of life's circumstances as opportunities to develop greater faith and stronger determination to live for God. Barbara was freed from her desire to control her circumstances, thus allowing God to work for good in every situation she was forced to endure.

There is no easy road to eternal life. We must not only have faith, but we must demonstrate our faith by depending on God to provide us with a sense of purpose even in the midst of "meaningless" tragedy. We must not let anything turn us away from Him.

### For Discussion

1. What has been the greatest tragedy of your life? Did

you plunge into despair and depression? How do Barbara's conclusions and the Scripture verses cited give you insight regarding your own problems?

2. Barbara says that even a great calamity does not protect us from other problems. Have you had that experience? Do continued problems and difficulties break down your composure, or do they provide opportunity for you to commit yourself more completely to God and draw more fully on His resources?

3. What does it mean to be a human being? Do we really have freedom in Christ? What is left to us when the life we live is destroyed by illness? Victor Frankl says that freedom for humans centers in our choosing how we will die—as saint or swine. How do you interpret his statement? What experiences in your life support or challenge your own conclusions?

4. After reading Barbara's story and recalling your own life, is there a song you would regard as your testimony? Does Barbara's song ring true in your life?

# CHAPTER 7

## Ellen

*Ellen Withrow, a devoted wife, worked at many jobs to help her husband complete his education in clinical psychology. Despite an eight-year battle with cancer, she made their home radiant with unselfish love. Ellen enjoyed her home and always regretted leaving it, especially for the frequent hospitalizations and operations she had to have. Here is her story in her own words.*

Our family included Jana and Jon; we had a new home in the San Fernando Valley of southern California where Quentin enjoyed his work as a clinical psychologist. With our third child, Joel, about to be born, we wondered how anyone could have a better life than we had. God's blessings had brought peace and tranquility into our section of the world.

When Joel was almost a year old, I found him dead in his crib. "Sudden infant death," the doctors called it. A little later, my mother underwent critical cancer surgery. Then I, too, developed a malignancy. I submitted to radical breast surgery, followed by twenty-five cobalt treatments. My father died of a sudden heart attack. I had another breast biopsy and a gall bladder operation. I developed brain cancer, a condition requiring five trips to the operating room in four weeks plus another twenty-five cobalt treatments.

Eventually I needed an operation to remove some malignant lymph glands.

Amid all those problems I developed back cancer. That again necessitated cobalt treatments and removal of my adrenal glands, complicated by acute kidney failure.

Failure showed in every organ of my body except my heart. I lapsed into a coma which lasted three weeks and was followed by another five weeks in the intensive care unit. All of this resulted in a $15,000 hospital bill, which did not include the physician's fee.

I list these experiences because they form the map of my pilgrimage. But my problems by no means represent the most difficult or tragic circumstances possible. Many people have suffered much more than I. I have simply compiled the events of my personal journey. I know I run the risk of your misunderstanding, your judgment, or your rejection. Yet I have committed myself to witness to God's presence in my life. My father, bless him, rarely passed up an opportunity to teach a lesson. Much of my odyssey, therefore, I too interpret as an experience from which I can learn.

The death of our little boy was the darkest hour of my life. Reconciliation with God did not come until a year and a half later while I was in the hospital following breast surgery. The lesson I learned from his death (it seems naive now) was that Christians are not immune from the tragedies of life. I had questioned, "Why did Joel have to die? After all, our home was Christian, and I had attended church almost every week of my life."

It seemed that God didn't care about me. I felt deserted and overwhelmed by anger, agony, and grief. Dozens of questions arose, but few answers emerged. It seemed as if the "cup" would never pass from me. Yet, as for Jesus in Gethsemane, the Father proved my shield and buffer. Christ gave me inner strength.

I have learned that God comes to me and ministers to my needs through the love and concern of my friends. Many people allowed goodness and mercy to work through them. They opened themselves to God's commission to love their neighbors. Other people were "Marthas" and set about preparing meals for our family. Thirty-two units of blood were given by church people and by men from the Christian Center, a home for people who had no other home. Many people prayed, and some fasted.

### Lessons To Be Learned

Radical breast surgery is an operation that brings with it implications beyond the physical loss. Each time before going to the hospital I have a sort of cleansing ceremony. I set my hair and paint my fingernails, even though I know that someone will shave my hair and remove my nail polish. I take a shower and scrub until I am "squeaky clean." The more scared I am, the harder I scrub. This cleansing seems necessary, because I do not like to look down over a white sheet and see grubby toes.

But on that occasion, before my mastectomy, standing looking in the mirror, I knew I would never see my body complete again.

Then the following conversation unfolded in my mind: "Ellen, you know what? Physical loss can be spiritual gain. You're just going to have to be a better person with only one breast!" I came to believe that lesson strongly: Our losses can help us make gains.

Next came a lesson on values. Which is worth more—a complete body or the opportunity to witness, especially to my children? With God's help I would not be defeated by my circumstances.

Later I learned a lesson of acceptance. Complete acceptance of a problem seldom came the first time I prayed about it. I compare my acceptance of something to going up hill, then down, and finally coasting into a kind of peace with reality. I accept that situation without apologies or self-pity, but with openness and humor. Having experienced those difficult circumstances, I can empathize with other pilgrims.

Another aspect of acceptance included gratitude—for the aspirin, clean sheets, ice water. Obviously, many people around the world suffer from illnesses like mine without being able to take even a single aspirin. Gratitude for those small comforts provided a healing balm for me.

I went home from the breast operation in ten days, without even a bandage. One of my friends commented, "What a strong constitution you have. You really recover fast." I accepted that as God's goodness. But I lacked the strength and wisdom to say the words "God healed me."

I hardly recognized that I was being healed. As a child, I was taught that God healed instantaneously and miraculously. I expected, therefore, that my own healing would be immediate and total. That did not happen. Therefore I was quite cautious about discussing healing with others; I feared not being healed myself, and I did not want to make other pilgrims question their faith. Secretly I felt there would be plenty of time to talk about healing after I had been pronounced "cured" after five years.

Frequently I prayed with little faith. I just shared my needs with God, expecting little or nothing in return, wanting mostly to verbalize my concerns and hoping that He would listen. When that "help yourself" kind of faith failed, I learned another lesson. Until our faith moves beyond self-preservation, beyond the faith that preserves only a questionable sanity in this broken world; until life stretches us; until we pray earnestly; until we pray without ceasing for resources beyond ourselves—we are only on the fringe of "living by faith."

**Another Round**
Three years later I began getting headaches. Within a month I couldn't move my head without acute pain. I entered Robert Long Hospital in Indianapolis. After a week of tests and medication my excruciating head pains stopped. My spirits rose. I believed that the relief had come from God and medicine. Then on a Sunday evening after visiting hours, the neurosurgeon came to my room. Kindness was evident in his careful and patient answers to my many questions, but he spoke no strong words of encouragement. Finally he said: "If it is operable. . . ." I heard very few of his words after that—I had brain cancer. He scheduled me for brain surgery a fews days later.

After the operation, when I awoke in the intensive care unit, I couldn't see. The tumor had involved the visual area of my brain, and the surgeon could not remove all of it. Before surgery I had been assured that my vision would be nearly normal. Now I couldn't even feed myself. A very thoughtful nurse fed me my favorite dish, chili. Whoever heard of a patient in the intensive care unit getting chili for her first meal? At least something functioned correctly—my taste buds.

The women's cancer ward of an old, dreary hospital in a big, dirty city is not my choice of places to have a deep spiritual experience. With my head shaved and a still-obvious incision the size and shape of a horseshoe, I nonetheless experienced a healing of my soul. I was not concerned with what was happening to me or happening around me; I felt bold, and I experienced a new communion with God. He and I were in perfect fellowship.

Soon, however, I was to learn another lesson. Although God had healed my soul and mind and all seemed well, I knew I could not stay on that "mountaintop" forever. Sometime soon I would come down off that spiritual cloud nine. I prayed for His peace and presence when that time would come. It came, and He answered my prayers more abundantly than I had asked.

Still, doubt remained my companion when it came to the subject of physical healing. I knew so many beautiful people who had led productive lives but who had suffered slow, agonizing deaths. If God did not heal them, how could I presume to ask for healing?

On Thanksgiving Day I located an oblong lump on my lower neck. Reluctantly I went back to the hospital and off to the operating room.

Sometime later I was resting quietly and chatting with my husband, when the physician called him to the door. "The lymph gland I removed from her neck is malignant," he said. "I found several areas of tumor on her back also. Cancer has her now for sure." I had crossed that bridge in my mind; now I had to cross it in reality.

In order to treat the cancer in my neck and back I underwent X-ray treatments. When I finished the first treatment period and packed my suitcase to go home for Christmas, I knew I would be back again in a month. The joy of Christmas season with my family in Oklahoma City helped push aside the awful feeling: *I am condemned.* The evidence of malignancies in two more areas helped us decide to proceed with adrenal surgery. The adrenalectomy, an operation to ease but not cure, might discourage the further spread of cancer.

I searched my soul. I felt my own unworthiness for healing. I prayed and prayed for many things, but never once did I pray "Heal me." Then, in the stillness of a sleepless night I whispered, "God, maybe You would . . . maybe You could heal me." It was a fragile and faint prayer, but my faith had stretched again. His peace and His presence surrounded me. At times I have wished for the "tongues of angels," but never more than then.

Nightmarish thoughts—hallucinations, delusions, visions, dreams—paraded through my mind during the three-week coma that followed adrenal surgery. The fantastic voyage of my mind, the imaginings so diverse and detailed, still seem unbelievable.

In one horrifying delusion a robot world appeared. I saw myself as the only human in that weird world, with soulless objects reaching out to push and pull my body and take parts of it away. No doubt some actual experience triggered many of those thoughts: A breathing apparatus forced air in and out of my lungs; a kidney dialysis machine attached to several tubes in my abdomen forced fluid in and out of my body. Tubes protruded from my nose, mouth, throat, neck, arms, and abdomen. My body swelled with fluid, turned yellow with liver stoppage, turned black and blue from internal bleeding.

For a time my blood system did not produce platelets, essential to blood coagulation. My skin cracked and peeled from dehydration. Only my heart continued to function properly. Real and imagined terrors plagued me. I now interpret that coma as God's mercy. Very little pain registered in my mind.

Finally I awoke to hear my mother's voice move from out

in space closer and closer until she appeared as a real person, standing by my bed. The physician standing beside her asked me, "What is your name?"

I couldn't answer.

"Where are you?"

I was in a hospital in Indianapolis. I was glad I knew it. He directed me to hold up two fingers. I could do that, and communication started.

When roused completely from the coma, I became aware of my critical condition. All those awful tubes. It seemed as if cement filled my body. I couldn't move. I was cold and hungry. Thirst overcame me. With my wrists tied to the sides of the bed, I felt completely helpless.

My physicians had no medical "road map." By their own admission I was the most critical patient they had ever treated, so complex were my problems. Five or six physicians worked around the clock. We came to love the surgeon, for his concern, enthusiasm, sharing, honesty. He told my husband, and me later, that his family had prayed for our family.

### "Great Is Thy Faithfulness"

Altogether, I came through a rare and remarkable experience. Five weeks after I came home from the hospital, I drove the ninety-mile round trip to the Indianapolis airport. My surgeon had indicated that such a venture would be impossible until at least five months hence.

By now you must be asking yourself, "Did God heal her? Does she think she's healed, if she's had cancer in so many areas?"

I've had those thoughts too. I believe that God *is* healing me. Present tense. I believe that God's creating and sustaining plan is perfect. I believe that our bodies are designed as a part of that plan. Every minute of our lives, awake or asleep, biochemical forces recycle our blood and rebuild our tissues. Metabolic forces cleanse and restore every part of our body. There is much we do not understand, but God *is* healing until our brain ceases to function and we draw our last breath.

Something else happened that testified to me about the mighty God we serve. While I watched a television program broadcast from space, I saw a small thing about the size of a baseball, and blue. And then the announcer said, "There's the earth."

That blue ball gave me an overwhelming sense of the reality of God. A blue ball—bathed in solar energy and held in place by gravity, with millions of trees and shrubs, flowers and plants, birds in the sky, animals on the land, fish in the water; thousands of rivers, lakes, valleys, mountains; seas and polar caps. And that blue ball is like a grain of sand in God's universe.

God is healing. God is the Creator. God is the Sustainer. Yes, and more. When you have prayed until there seem to be no more prayers, when you have questions and find no answers, when you have cried until there seem to be no more tears, say it. Say from deep inside you this simple affirmation: *God is.* That is sufficient. He has no limitations, and He requires no definitions. God is, and you are His, and He is yours. God is our destiny, if we so choose.

*We Have An Eternal Home*
*Read 2 Corinthians 4:16—5:8.*

Two years after telling her story, Ellen Withrow died. Pastor Collins began the funeral service by reading from 2 Corinthians 4:7–11:

But we have this treasure in earthen vessels, to show that the transcendent power belongs to God and not to us. We are afflicted in every way, but not crushed; perplexed, but not driven to despair; persecuted, but not forsaken; struck down, but not destroyed; always carrying in the body the death of Jesus, so that the life of Jesus may also be manifested in our bodies. For while we live we are always being given up to death for Jesus' sake, so that the life of Jesus may be manifested in our mortal flesh.

Pastor Collins continued, "This Scripture tells us of a mystery, the mystery that these earthen vessels we call bodies may contain the transcendent glory of God. Occasionally I meet a person whose earthen vessel has thin places in the walls that allow the light of God's glory to shine through. Because God's glory shines through those thin places in their lives, we know better what God is like. Ellen Withrow was one of those rare persons.

"During the years of her illness, Ellen talked a lot about healing. She came back from the brink of death after her most critical operation and went on to lead a vigorous, beautiful, incredibly productive life.

"I saw God operating in Ellen through an inexplicable combination, an intense love for life and a fearlessness of death. On one occasion I passed her family physician on the street. He said to me, 'There are two things that keep Ellen alive. One is her faith in God; the other is her determination to live.' Probably nobody ever fought more resolutely against greater odds, to stay alive.

"At one point, doctors at Indiana University commented, 'Ellen is the most critical patient we've had who survived.' She won the battle for life again and again. It's no wonder her doctors loved her. Ellen and God made them look good!

"Ellen Withrow told a story of God's presence and help—not after she had solved the problems of fear, anger, and doubt, but in the midst of them. She did not believe that

Ellen

God had to be defended with smooth clichés. She believed that telling the truth glorifies Him. 'There have been times,' she said, 'when fear, like an angry animal, gnawed at my insides. At times my cup ran over and over and over. Often a tiredness or hurt cried deep inside me. Yet when I reached out to Jesus, He gave me wholeness and peace.' "

*For Discussion*

1. Ellen Withrow said she experienced healing even on her deathbed. How do you understand her remark?

2. Ellen also said that Christians have no insurance against the tragedies of life. Write down some of the problems you have encountered, both before and after you became a Christian. Can you think of any "saints" who suffer terrible illnesses or any evil people who enjoy good health?

3. How important is the complete health of your body to you? Do you consider anything more valuable than a healthy body? Would you feel that God loved you more if He were to heal you quickly when you were significantly ill or if He were to lead you to inner wholeness *through* your suffering?

4. Have you ever been seriously ill? If so, what changes occurred in your relationship with God because of it? Recall both good and bad results. Do you think you grew through the experience, or did it defeat you?

5. Is the true meaning of life different when we are helplessly sick as opposed to being fully well? What does life mean to you?

6. What basic relationship with God did Ellen express? Think about your relationship to God. Do you serve God because of what He does or for who He is?

# PART TWO

## TWO

### A Doctor's View of Healing

# CHAPTER 8
## The Miracle of Wholeness

Most of us need to refine our definition of what a miracle actually is. People use the word *miracle* to describe all kinds of events. We hear that word when a football halfback climbs over an entire opposing team to score a touchdown, or when an impossible catch is made by a baseball outfielder. When people walk away unharmed from an automobile crash that totally destroyed a car, we shake our heads and say "It's a miracle they survived!" A spaceship safely carries astronauts to the moon and back, and that, too, is described as a miracle.

Such confused or careless use of the word even invades our theology. As a result, many people struggle in their relationship to God. I find in my medical practice that the incorrect use of the term *miracle* causes more difficulty than almost any other problem. If I didn't know otherwise, from the way many Christians talk, I would have to conclude that God works in this world mainly by means of so-called miracles.

I believe that the only scientifically-documented, true miracle I have ever witnessed was the transformation in the life of my infant daughter (see Chapter 2). I have been told that I was healed by direct, instantaneous, divine healing of congenital heart disease when I was a blue baby. As I try to recall instances of miracles in the lives of my patients, I think of the individual with an X-ray-proven cancer of the colon who was healed the night before surgery by prayer, so that at the time of the operation the next day, the cancer was gone. On another occasion I had to graft a four-year-old girl's third-degree-burned face; I had never performed such an operation before. I prayed for God's help, and the Holy Spirit guided my hands in producing a face that was still pretty after the healing.

When we use simplistic definitions, however, we can easily make a miracle an everyday event in which God jumps from situation to situation around the world to change or break His laws so that the needs of His children can be met. On one hand, if we pursue this type of thinking, we get ourselves into a blind alley where God is working against His own laws and rules of life on planet earth. On the other hand, this recklessness with the word *miracle* can lead us into assuming that God acts at our beck-and-call, which means that we practice religious magic. Furthermore, religious magic can parade as a miracle as easily as the chameleon can change its colors.

### What Is a Miracle?

*Webster's New Collegiate Dictionary* defines *miracle* as (1) an extraordinary event manifesting divine intervention in human affairs; (2) an extremely outstanding or unusual event, thing, or accomplishment.[6] Religious people quite generally believe that in order for an event to qualify as a miracle it must manifest the supernatural power of God.

Sometimes calling something miraculous in actuality means that we don't have all the facts or fully understand the situation. In addition, what appears to be a miracle to one society may be explained differently by another. I recall a story about a man who visited an Indian tribe. The Indians were about to kill him; he pleaded with them and told them that if they would wait three days he would make the moon stop shining. When it happened as he predicted, he was celebrated as a god. The Indians did not understand that an eclipse of the moon had occurred.

In our own culture, we see how the outstanding progress of today's technology renders the transplanting of human kidneys and hearts not miraculous but commonplace. And a visit to Universal City Studios in Hollywood reveals that the special effects we see on television programs are not miracles but twentieth-century sleight-of-hand.

*Remission or Miracle?* Within a short period of time I operated on two patients and in each man found an inoperable abdominal cancer. One patient had a remarkable recovery and was able to return to work. His strength gradually became normal, and the symptoms of his cancer disappeared. Even the yellow coloring in his eyes went away. Because he and his friends continually prayed for his full recovery, his family and friends said, "A miracle has happened!"

The other man had a similar experience. His cancer likewise went into remission. However, neither he nor his family ever prayed for a miracle or for healing. Afterward, they did not say that a miracle had taken place. Both of the men died about ten months after their operations.

Doctors cannot explain why some patients have dramatic remissions of their disease. Chemotherapy, improved nutrition, spontaneous regression of the tumor, or some direct action by God may contribute to the phenomenon of remission. But is it a miracle of healing, or is it a temporary change? In all cases, however long or short the duration of healing, I give God the glory. No healing can ever occur unless the healing power of God repairs the body.

When we see a sunrise or sunset or the sparkling Milky

Way on a clear night, we exclaim, "Oh, the greatness of God's handiwork!" We sense the power of God, and rightly so. His creative genius arouses our awe. The bountiful beauty of nature assures us of His love for us and presence with us. Even so, nature cannot interact with us; there is no communication. Yet we long for dialogue with our Maker and God.

In the same way, the healing of a broken leg only symbolizes His presence in and concern for our lives. When God heals a broken leg He does not become part of the molecules or tissues of the restored bone. As with nature, physical healing, then, may be only a sign or illustration of God's presence. Although we do not understand exactly how God heals, the word miracle does not actually fit when we talk about God directly healing the sick body. All creation, which of course includes our bodies, obeys the Creator's voice. When God commanded the formation of heaven and earth and the appearance of the plants and animals, nature obeyed His will. The response of nature to God's command, therefore, is standard operating procedure for the physical universe.

*Magic or Miracle?* A patient of mine once articulated a lack of distinction between miracles and magic: "Doctor, I hear that you are a Christian physician, which makes me very glad because I want you to pray for me. Pray that everything will go well while you are operating on me. I want to be sure that everything will be perfectly all right."

Although that young woman felt keenly about God's ability to perform a miracle in her body, she was asking me to do something for her that only God could do. As physicians, Christian or otherwise, we have no way of manipulating God. I appreciated the confidence she had in me and her acknowledgment that I am a Christian, but she needed to communicate with God herself. The Bible tells us to pray for each other, and I am always happy to pray with and for my patients. But if I had done what I thought she was asking for, I would have been playing God, and we would have been deceiving ourselves.

In Ellen Withrow's story (Chapter 7), after one of her many operations she stated that her relief from pain had come from God *and* medicine. A doctor often wishes that more patients would show such balance.

In the New Testament, Luke, a physician, described the confusion existing then in the minds of people over whether something should be called magical or miraculous (see Acts 8:9-24). Simon, a sorcerer known for his ability to bewitch people *before* he became a believer, was held in high regard. We are told that he was amazed at the signs and miracles performed by the apostle Philip. The people had thought that Simon's great power came from God. After becoming a believer, when Simon saw what happened as a result of the apostles' laying on of hands, he offered money to Peter and John, asking them to ". . .'Give me also this power, that any one on whom I lay my hands may receive the Holy Spirit' " (v. 19). Peter responded with a rebuke: ". . .'Your silver perish with you, because you thought you could obtain the gift of God with money!' " (v. 20).

Miracles become a problem when we seek for physical signs instead of for God Himself. At some point in life, perhaps most of us are tempted to indulge in a little wishful thinking, if not to invite the spirit of magic. Dr. Paul Tournier says:

> The spirit of magic lies in wait for the Christians as much as for the agnostics and the pagans. It arises, in fact, from an inherent tendency in human nature, and none of us can boast of being proof

against its wiles. It is the longing for the fairy tale, for the magic wand that will charm away the difficulties of life, the suffering, the limitations, and the uncertainties of our human condition.[7]

We see that longing in those who believe they can master life by simply finding the correct words, incantation, or activity which they can then repeat at will. Tournier further emphasizes:

A subtle temptation consists in trying to use magically the gifts of God Himself, His own promises, the faith He has given us, the experiences He has granted us, the Bible He has inspired, and the dogma He revealed. In the account of Jesus in the wilderness being tempted by the Devil, it is God's promises that are used. The Devil quotes the Scripture in an attempt to awaken in Jesus the apparently legitimate ambition to demonstrate in some striking way the power He possesses in order to sway the multitudes. Jesus replies that this would be to tempt God.[8]

Most Christians oppose any implication that prayers for healing are, in the final analysis, "religious magic" or "superstitious." But if we fall into a line of reasoning that insists that the healing of our bodies is proof of God's favor, we may be coming close to superstition and magic. At times people so earnestly seek healing by the Lord that when their bodies are not healed miraculously they are convinced God must not care for them. They lose faith in Him, seeing the promises of Jesus as merely the words of a man.

Over and over again in the New Testament account of Jesus' life we see people pestering Him for a "sign" and following Him in the hope that they would see Him perform miracles. But He couldn't be coerced that way. To the Pharisees who sought from Him "a sign from heaven" (Mark

8:11), Jesus said, ". . . No sign shall be given . . ." (v. 12).

As a physician, I have seen patients dying of cancer who would not admit their terminal condition. Such an admission, they believed, would demonstrate a lack of faith in God's ability to heal. Until the day they die, some people maintain that position. Their religious "incantations" are as predictable as the familiar Bible verses they repeat to "claim" healing.

In such instances I have observed the pain inflicted on family members who did not necessarily hold their loved one's view. Not that these relatives didn't believe God could perform a miracle; the reality of the situation simply showed them the need, at that juncture, to accept what was happening. Not all are healed in this life. Sometimes the greater healing is in the mind, as one accepts with true grace the fact that God is greater than our infirmities and that He knows what is happening.

### Toward a Proper View of Miracles

A word used carelessly loses its meaning. One woman complained that her husband had the habit of calling waitresses "Dear," so now when he calls her "Dear," it doesn't convey anything special. The word *love* is another example. We "love" ice cream, and we "love" our mates. How much that word has been misused.

So it is with the word *miracle*. We Christians have unwittingly erected a barrier in the minds of non-Christians with our casual use of that word. Non-Christians often think Christians see God working only through miracles. Logically, however, that type of miracle-thinking arises from a deistic concept of God, rather than from the biblical revelation of God. Some Christians seem to believe that God made the world, hurled it into space, and abandoned it, occasionally returning to perform a miracle to remind us of His power and presence.

Such a philosophy has been called the "craftsman model." Malcolm A. Jeeves explains it this way.

> According to this thought-model, God the Creator is conceived as an infinitely wise and clever inventor and constructor, who has, at some point in time, produced the universe as we know it and has set it running. It is usually also implied that once the machine has been set running, it is to all intents and purposes autonomous, except for very occasional interventions when some particular event has to be brought about or some servicing of the machine is required.
>
> Such a view leads to a false kind of supernaturalism, in that it suggests that God's activity in the created world should be looked for and discerned mainly in occasional acts from without, which are injected into the otherwise autonomous orderly working of the machine.
>
> In short, models of this kind encourage a philosophy of nature which regards it simply as an autonomous machine which needs no divine sustaining activity to keep it in existence from moment to moment. So for God to bring about events which are commonly considered to be miraculous, He must return and intervene in a system which He has previously set going and then left.[9]

Yet the Bible constantly assures us that God continues to be in His world, moment by moment.

### TV Healers

Much of what we see on televised healing programs may be magic instead of miracles. The faith healers who televise their healing "miracle" programs usually emphasize mass healings. Frequently the viewer sees an assembly-line approach which leaves little time for any one individual. The faith healer, not even knowing the person's name, usually has no true knowledge of the person's condition or motives for desiring healing. Instead, quite contrary to Jesus' own approach, the healer uses routine gestures and phrases.

Emphasis in such services typically centers on a dramatic physical change, often instantaneous, instead of on the whole person—body, mind, and soul. The healer almost commands God to heal: "Now in the name of Jesus. . . ." Some pull the sickness out of the person's ears; others knock down the sick one. During one televised program a faith healer said, "All I have to do is say 'Jesus' three times, and people are healed."

Although such services have been conducted for many years, there is little evidence that they have accomplished anything truly or eternally helpful to people. Yes, many have been made physically better. But what about the other elements of their personality? Are they any further along their pilgrimage of faith in Jesus Christ when the tragedies of life and death strike later?

Many of the people who are not healed express a loss of faith or a decreased closeness to God. That whole approach, therefore, presents a contradiction of faith to thousands of people. Because miracles are described in physical terms as signs of God's love and presence, those who aren't experiencing those signs feel inadequate in their relationship with God.

The "have your miracle today" approach emphasizes the created rather than the Creator. It has minimized fellowship with Christ by its excessive stress on the physical.

Although that approach to miracles has been profitable financially, bringing multimillion-dollar incomes to some healers, it has produced little understanding of the love of God. The secular world emphasizes the body and encourages us to enjoy our bodies, to live for the body. But the Bible says that we cannot go to heaven with these finite bodies (see 1 Cor. 15). Such singular emphasis on the physical body is counterproductive to a life of faith and eternal life. Paul reminds us that our bodies are the temple of God (see 1 Cor. 3:16). To identify a miracle as that which happens to our bodies, therefore, misses the whole point of God's interaction with the world. Transcendence goes beyond the body to the spiritual: the inner person.

What, then, can be said about miracles? Miracles do not necessarily violate, suspend, or contradict laws of nature. God authors both miracles and nature. God has the power, therefore, to accomplish His purposes over a period of time or instantaneously; He may blend the forces of the universe any way He desires. Possibly He allows certain events to happen by changing the dominance of the powers He established when He created the cosmos. We do not know. God is not bound by our human understanding of nature. He may have made the universe such that miracles are the purpose of nature. Undoubtedly the only miracle that is worthy of all nature is the Incarnation of God into human life.

### Central Miracle

The preeminent miracle is the Incarnation of the eternal Son of God. Incarnation means "in-flesh-ment." C. S. Lewis said

... the central miracle asserted by Christians is the Incarnation. They say that God became Man. Every other miracle prepares for this, or exhibits this, or results from this. Just as every natural event is the manifestation at a particular place and moment of Nature's total character, so every particular Christian miracle manifests at a particular place and moment the character and significance of the Incarnation. [10]

Elton Trueblood states it this way:

> If we find ourselves unable to believe in miracles, we may still think of God as the Author of the universe, including its natural laws, but such belief is almost valueless for practical religion. There does not seem much reason for worshipping a God who has made a world such that he is effectually shut out from participation in its management.[11]

Jesus, the Word of God, became flesh and lived for thirty-three years among other human beings. His birth, life, crucifixion, and resurrection form the Incarnation, the greatest miracle. All other miraculous events must reflect the Incarnation, or we are moving toward magic.

One way of stating the difference between miracles and magic might be this: Miraculous events reflect the Creator; magic emphasizes the created.

Although our relationship with God often includes what God does for us as we petition Him with our needs, an essential miracle occurs when the Spirit of Jesus Christ finds a place in our lives. That brings the Incarnation home, so to speak, for each human being.

The adjective *miraculous*, then, would pertain to all those wonderful events in which we see God at work in physical life. By restricting the noun *miracle* to the Incarnation but using the adjective *miraculous* for all evidences of God at work in creation, we would always be emphasizing God, the Creator, rather than nature or people, the created. The one great miracle unfolds when we love God, serve Him, and commune with Him. The apostle Paul said, ". . . I consider everything a loss compared to the surpassing greatness of knowing Christ Jesus my Lord. . ." (Phil. 3:8 NIV).

It is not that miraculous deeds prove the divinity of

Christ; rather, Christ bears witness that what He does is miraculous. He did not call attention to Himself, gather a crowd, perform a miraculous healing, and then ask people to follow Him. As he quietly encountered individual men and women at the level of their needs, they became aware of their healed bodies and spirits. John S. Bonnell came to a similar conclusion in his book *Do You Want to Be Healed?*

Theologians of earlier centuries sometimes regarded the miracles of Jesus as a kind of seal or proof of the authenticity of his person and ministry. Not a few people in our time take the same view, as though our Lord needed something in addition to his incomparable life and teaching to validate his ministry. These remarkable healings they think were made to draw attention to Jesus and to personally exalt him. They were his credentials to convince the doubting, testimonials to persuade the unbelieving.

If we study the Gospel records, however, we see that they flatly contradict this viewpoint. Actually he shrank from publicity. Deliberately, he sought to avoid the crowd. In the temptation in the wilderness, Jesus completely rejected any thought of using startling and dramatic displays to win people to his kingdom. The motivation for his healing lay in his all-consuming desire to make them whole.[12]

Why did Jesus perform miraculous works? They were part of the expression of God *in* His world: God was in Christ reconciling the world to Himself. The appropriate response to Jesus' miraculous healings was always repentance and faith in that Good News. His miraculous works focused not so much on the comfort of some person's body as on spiritual truth. Whenever we encounter Jesus Christ as our Lord and Savior, we have witnessed the essence of miracle. Dietrich Bonhoeffer summed it up like this:

Only the believing community recognizes the approach of the kingdom in the miracles of Jesus. It does not see only magic and false claims here. . . . The unbeliever says, "Here is the kingdom of God" . . . . the believer sees in it the prelude to the divine action at the end of the world. But the non-believer sees nothing.[13]

Since nonbelievers do not understand the Creator-created relationship, they cannot see the miracle, only the magic. To see the miraculous, one must see the Christ. We see Him only by faith, and what is faith but an openness to God? ". . . faith is the assurance of things hoped for, the conviction of things not seen" (Heb. 11:1). Central to faith is the understanding that God created the world by His Word.

### Keeping Miracles Christ-Centered

We do not demonstrate faith simply by claiming that we believe in miracles. Bonhoeffer again spoke clearly.

There is only faith where a man so surrenders himself to the humiliated God-man as to stake his life on him, even when this seems against all sense. Faith is where the attempt to have security from something visible is rejected. In that case, it is faith in God and not in the world. The only assurance that faith tolerates is the Word itself which comes to me through Christ.[14]

Faith affirms that God loves me so much that regardless of any situations I face I can trust Him, confident that He will not forsake me but commune with me. Faith grows through our communion with Christ. Eugenia Price, in her study of crises and tragedies, concluded:

Dare we depend upon "miracles" to dispel our doubts? Is this the ultimate test of faith? Isn't the main issue God Himself? And don't we ignore Him when we search wildly for specific answers to our specific sorrows? I am on safe ground only when I direct attention to Jesus Christ Himself.[15]

Scripture records God's purpose in the miracle of the Incarnation in John 3:16,17 (NEB): " 'God loved the world so much that he gave his only Son, that everyone who has faith in him may not die but have eternal life. It was not to judge the world that God sent his Son into the world, but that through him the world might be saved.' "

The purpose of that great miracle helps us grasp the fundamental concept of wholeness for human beings: "Therefore, if anyone is in Christ, he is a new creation; old things have passed away; behold, all things have become new. And all things are of God, who has reconciled us to Himself through Jesus Christ, and has given us the ministry of reconciliation" (2 Cor. 5:17,18 NKJB-NT).

How do we receive the miracle? By faith in Jesus Christ. Not by works. We don't deserve it, and we cannot buy it. But by the grace of God we can have the miracle of wholeness by responding to God's love for us. We can concentrate our time, thoughts, money, and actions on developing a right relationship with Jesus Christ.

Our natural response to the miracle of having a special relationship to God is gratitude and praise. Our life of praise should encourage others to respond to Christ and should bear the fruit of His Spirit in our interpersonal relationships.

The miracle of Christ in our life results in what the Bible calls the "abundant life." Since Christ is the Source of truth, we find fulfillment, meaning, and significance in Him. Our relationship with others deepens, becoming worthwhile and healthy because He is our intermediary. He provides for "I-Thou" encounters instead of merely "I-It" experiences.

# The Miracle of Wholeness

Thus we become harmonious members of the "body of Christ" on earth. As the Spirit of the incarnate Christ abides in us and expresses Himself through us, we find fulfillment of our personhood because the image of God is in us. We *can* become the person He created us to be.

The comments of a sixty-year-old woman with cancer of the uterus, who underwent radium and cobalt therapy in preparation for a hysterectomy, reveal the kind of faith in Jesus Christ I am talking about. Faith provided her with a firm place to stand when the ground of her being was shaken. In an interview before the operation she told me:

I am totally committed to the will of God. Whether I receive physical healing or not is not the issue. Whichever way God can work best is my concern. If anyone would be saved through my illness, then even having cancer would be worthwhile for me. For me to live is Christ, and to die for Him is gain. Whether I live or die under these circumstances, I'll win over this apparent tragedy.

The night before the radium implantation I was alone. Suddenly, I had a vision of Jesus, my Lord. He said, "I'll never leave you." I recalled the account of Jesus in the garden of Gethsemane when He felt so alone and forsaken. Now I see Him as more human, and yet I appreciate His divinity more too.

I don't know what I will have to face in life, but I do know that if I keep close to God, He will commune with me, whatever happens, and give me the resources I will need to face tomorrow.

### For Discussion

1. How have you been defining *miracle*? Have you ever experienced a miracle, or do you know a person who has?

2. Can you outline what a miracle is, based on what has been said in this chapter? Include the purpose, the receiving, the response to, and the result of miracle. Now apply

this definition to some of the miracles you know about. Have you been helped to see Christ more clearly?

3. Discuss the difference between miracle and magic. Make a list of the points you think belong under each heading. What can you add to that list which would allow you to explain the difference to a Christian? To a non-Christian?

4. If we call extraordinary physical events miracles and say that miracles exist to show God's mighty power, what might that definition of miracle imply about God when He does not perform such a miracle?

5. In the last chapter of the Book of Job, God restored Job's physical wealth *after* Job prayed for Him to restore his friends who had been so troublesome to Job. What was the great miracle in Job's life?

6. Talk with a non-Christian friend about miracles. Ask that person which definition of miracle discussed above could cause him or her to consider becoming a Christian.

# CHAPTER 9

## Is There Meaning in Suffering?

Why suffering, death, and tragedy exist has plagued humankind over the centuries. I do not pretend to know or understand all the *whys*. But as a Christian, a physician, and a patient, I believe tragedies can be overcome through faith in Jesus Christ.

The problem of sickness, suffering, and death began in the Garden of Eden. God had created the earth and made a paradise for Adam and Eve. He intended them to live in the fullness of paradise and in daily communion with Him in an unblemished world. But their choice to disobey God resulted in a world of decay, deterioration, and death.

Each of us represents Adam and Eve in the sense that we are part of humanity. If given the opportunity they had, we would no doubt have chosen as they did, for we also disobey God's commands. We, too, partake of the sinful nature of the human race. Because of Adam and Eve's choice, all of life reflects imperfection. But even though Adam and Eve brought chaos into the world, God ordained that He would use all things for our good. God is still very much concerned about His world and our roles in it. God created a universe in which we can discover the basic laws of life and create things that will help ease our living in this imperfect world. Consequently we can build homes that not only shelter us from heat and cold, storms and bad weather, but provide a center of family activity to help us grow and develop. There can be design rather than randomness, order rather than chaos, regularity rather than irregularity, law rather than anarchy, method rather than confusion, harmony rather than disharmony. The imperfections in life call our attention to the need for perfection. Such perfection is personified in Christ.

Even in sickness or other tragedy we can see God's loving concern for us. Most diseases, for instance, exhibit basic designs which allow the doctor to diagnose and treat them. Because of this uniformity, medical science has been able to develop specific treatments which are standard around the world. Dependable laws of tissue and organ deterioration and healing allow us to design operations and medications for most illnesses.

Acute appendicitis is one example. The appendix is a small appendage extending from the first two inches of the large bowel. As far as we know today, it serves no function in the human body. When the appendix becomes infected, specific signs and symptoms can usually be counted on to allow a physician to diagnose that disease. If the signs and symptoms of acute appendicitis were not constant, but changed from time to time, most people would die from it. Instead we are able to diagnose and operate in time on almost every person with acute appendicitis.

We have also developed antibiotics to fight the specific bacteria that cause acute appendicitis. At the time of the operation we can check a sample of the pus from the infected area and determine which antibiotics will control or destroy those particular bacteria.

Even with diseases for which we have no cure, generally we can treat a patient to keep the disease in check. The patient car resume at least some activities, although he or she may still have the disease. Sometimes we can prolong lives for months or years.

God gives us the ability to treat many physical and psychological illnesses, and He also uses these problems and sufferings to help us become better persons. One patient who had undergone two operations said that because of her sickness she and her husband reset their priorities. They found that when they put Christ in the center of their lives they could work out better solutions to their problems.

When we look at difficulties from the perspective of God's loving concern, we don't have to find a personal reason for every problem in our life. Part of what it means to be human is to live in a body and a universe that are imperfect and that therefore will decay and die. The illnesses and tragedies of life are part of the fabric of our existence and come to us simply because we are human, regardless of who we are, what we believe, or the way we act. Some problems, of course, do result specifically from breaking God's moral or physical laws.

One of my patients said, "There is some good that comes from every bad experience." We have to be willing, however, to see the potential for good and to allow God to use it to our benefit. God has not deserted us when hardship strikes. Whatever the problem, we can gain from it if we choose to do so.

Success in struggles comes when we creatively, thoughtfully search for strength in spite of a tragedy. Dr. V. Raymond Edman, former chancellor of Wheaton College in Illinois and a prolific writer, was fond of stating, "Not somehow, but triumphantly." With that kind of perspective a person can look at suffering not as an enemy but as an opportunity to develop faith in God. That is what Andraé

Crouch meant in his song, "Through It All": "If I'd never had a problem, I wouldn't know that He could solve them, I'd never know what faith in God could do."* Times of testing not only increase our faith but should promote a desire to commune with God for who He is rather than for what He can do for us. To see His faithfulness even in the worst tragedy is a blessing.

Sickness helps us discover the limitations of our human existence. We see where we stand in the universe. We are not the Creator but the created. Illness shows us that ultimately we are not in control of life or even of our own bodies—but we can control our attitudes and direct our responses.

### Suffering in the Bible

The Bible is full of examples of men and women who learned the lessons from suffering that God intended for them. David portrayed that dramatically in the Psalms. He was in anguish over and over again; he voiced his doubts and aired his grievances. But he always hastened to acknowledge his need of God. He didn't give up on God. He triumphed over his tragedies by calling to mind God's mercy. Notice what he says in Psalm 13.

> How long, O LORD? Will you forget me
>    forever?
> How long will you hide your face
>    from me?
> How long must I wrestle with my
>    thoughts
> and every day have sorrow in my
>    heart? . . .

---

*© Copyright 1971 by Manna Music, Inc., 2111 Kenmere Ave., Burbank, CA 91504. International copyright secured. All rights reserved. Used by permission.

*Is There Meaning in Suffering?* 105

>   Look on me and answer, O LORD my
>     God. . . .
>   But I trust in your unfailing love;
>     my heart rejoices in your salvation.
>   I will sing to the Lord,
>     for he has been good to me (vv. 1–3,5,6 NIV).

One psalm after another has that pattern. David is telling us something. He reminds us, "The LORD tests the righteous . . ." (Ps. 11:5). Who? *The Lord.*

A basic premise of the Psalms is that humans are made in the image of God. But unless we develop our inner selves to reflect God's presence in us, we have not become what we could be. That developmental process, occurring throughout life, is particularly stimulated by the difficulties and problems we face. The most marvelous thing is, that although people have sinned against their Creator, God has not turned His face against them. Because of His love and mercy He does not wait for us to turn to Him but comes to us. Thus we can look at the disappointments of life as messengers calling us to examine our walk with God. Are we "on schedule" in our growth and development? Or would death now mean failure and eternal loss for us?

Facing the worst tragedy of His life, Jesus went to Gethsemane to pray:

> Then Jesus came with them to a place called Gethsemane, and said to the disciples, "Sit here while I go and pray over there." And He took with Him Peter and the two sons of Zebedee, and He began to be sorrowful and deeply distressed. Then He said to them, "My soul is exceedingly sorrowful, even to death. Stay here and watch with Me." And He went a little farther, fell on His face, and prayed, saying, "O My Father, if it is possible, let this cup pass from Me; nevertheless, not as I will, but as You will. . . .

He went away again a second time and prayed, saying, "O My Father, if this cup may not pass away from Me unless I drink it, Your will be done." And He came and found them asleep again, for their eyes were heavy. And He left them, went away again, and prayed the third time, saying the same words (Matt. 26:36–39; 42–44 NKJB-NT).

What lesson is here for us? Jesus pleaded three times for His Father to remove His problem. Those entreaties to God were not just a quick prayer. Jesus said, "My soul is exceedingly sorrowful, even to death." Jesus bared His soul to God. He struggled and pleaded.

Jesus called God "Abba, Father." That would be like my saying "dear Father," or "Daddy," or (as I affectionately call my dad) "Pop." When we have an intimate relationship with someone, we usually have special words to denote that closeness. In using the word *Abba*, Jesus drew as near to God as He could at that time. He and the Father were one—but in assuming a physical body, the Son of God laid aside His heavenly position to become a human being. The apostle Paul explained this in his letter to the Christians at Philippi.

Let this mind be in you which was also in Christ Jesus, who, being in the form of God, did not consider equality with God something to be grasped, but emptied Himself by taking the form of a servant, and coming in the likeness of men. And being found in appearance as a man, He humbled Himself and became obedient to the point of death, even the death of the cross (Phil. 2:5–8 NKJB-NT).

In His prayer in the Garden of Gethsemane, Jesus acknowledged God's power to change His situation if God wanted to. By asking for God's will above His own, however, Jesus chose to put His life in God's hands. Jesus, as a human being, so trusted and loved His Father that He gave up His own will and pleasure for God's purposes, trusting that God's will was best not only for Him but for all humanity.

What if Jesus had refused God's will and insisted on His own? His birth and life had already blessed hundreds of people. Many had believed in God because of His words and deeds. But He would not have fulfilled the purpose of His coming to earth if He had not accepted the cross. Jesus accepted God's will although He experienced the human feelings expressed in that prayer. Jesus gave His life, accomplishing the Father's will, and thereby made access to God's love possible for those who believe and accept Him. God came into human life and conquered evil and death.

Our relationship with the Father can likewise be an open dialogue in which we lay bare our soul's turmoil. God through His Son has experienced human life and been tempted and tried. He is a sympathetic Savior.

Therefore, in all things He was obligated to be made like His brethren, that He might be a merciful and faithful High Priest in things pertaining to God, to make propitiation for the sins of the people. For in that He Himself has suffered, being tempted, He is able to aid those who are tempted. . . .

For we do not have a High Priest who cannot sympathize with our weaknesses, but was in all points tempted as we are, yet without sin. Let us therefore come boldly to the throne of grace, that we may obtain mercy and find grace to help in time of need (Heb. 2:17,18; 4:15,16 NKJB-NT).

## Our Mission in Pain

Through a deep, rich dialogue with Christ our Savior who suffered as we do, we can find meaning in our tragedies. How does this happen?

1. Through tragedy we have an opportunity to share with others what Christ has done for us. Having our needs met

through Christ's all-sufficient power, we become able to relate to others at a depth otherwise unknown. We can be open about who we are or hope to be. As we reveal our pilgrimage to one another, we form the fellowship that can be found uniquely in the body of Christ. When others see what Christ is doing in our lives, they may have an initial encounter with Christ or have their faith revitalized.

Lloyd J. Ogilvie says: "It's in our relationships that we are the good news we seek to share. To love people is to let them love you: to let them love you is to let them know you; to let them know you is to be open about your hurts and hopes; to be open means to be vulnerable."[16] Before we can share the power of Christ, we must experience it.

2. Suffering allows Christ to be our Lord as well as Savior. We ask for healing, but even if He does not heal our sick bodies, He will heal our spirits. Acceptance of that fact is acknowledgment of His Lordship. We have the assurance that He remains in fellowship with us. Such a dynamic relationship with Christ not only makes this life worthwhile, but through it we can accept the inevitability of our physical death and know that we will be part of the final resurrection.

When we have a deep faith in Christ He will motivate and lead us through all our trials and difficulties. We can hear Him speak to us through our sufferings. Suffering permits a special kind of service on our part. We can serve others in their sickness and problems as doctors and nurses, or simply as ourselves. Suffering calls for a witness to the healing power of God, whether there is physical healing or not.

3. Suffering calls for communion with Christ and with others. As suffering or tragedy strips us of our strengths, we become more aware of the conditions of our hearts. Cynthia Kane, one of my patients, had widespread cancer which had progressed from the breast into every bone of her body. Yet

she testified that the last five years with cancer were worth more to her than any period in her life because of the closeness to God she found. The daily strength He gave her to get out of bed and get dressed despite constant pain, the insights she received, and the ministry she shared with many people who visited her all required a depth of communion with God that she never knew existed before she became ill. She knew she was ready to die. She knew she would see Him face to face and have fellowship with Him without the constant distraction of her suffering body.

4. Suffering calls for growth of the inner person. When the problems of life assail us and threaten to demoralize us, we can ask Christ to use those problems to help us mature, to help us understand the person we are, and to help us see the person we can become.

5. Suffering calls for reconciliation: restoration of body, mind, and spirit. We seek the healing of our body, and we pray in faith for healing (see James 5:14–16). Yet we earnestly desire the higher healing of our person, which allows us to climb above our suffering. The miracle of healing comes not so much through physical cure as through reconciliation with God through Christ. Suffering also offers opportunities for reconciliation with others.

6. Suffering calls for community response to the sufferer. This holds true for both the family and the church. The support of loving, concerned family and friends during our trials provides extra strength and courage. We experience more of God's care and love. God works through His people.

7. Suffering allows the Holy Spirit to work in us. When we are terribly sick, too sick even to know how to pray, the Holy Spirit intercedes for us (see Rom. 8:26,27).

8. Suffering calls for meaning in our trials, value in our humanity, and purpose in our choices. If we view suffering as

unfair and are embittered, we will find ourselves unable to trust God as He works out His plan for our lives. Yet if we desire to grow we need to dedicate ourselves to developing a dynamic faith in God. That kind of faith requires struggle.

To believe in Christ, whom we cannot see, when everything about us is so devastating, requires tremendous inner determination and strength. Perhaps it is the greatest struggle of our mortal lives, requiring the Spirit of Christ dwelling in us. Otherwise we fall prey to our lower nature and live for our bodies instead of for God. Faith in Jesus Christ is *the* resource which enables us to face suffering and win.

**For Discussion**

1. Do you agree that this is the best possible world to live in? Why or why not?

2. How would you attempt to improve world conditions and (A) still preserve freedom of choice, or (B) keep people responsible for their desires and choices?

3. What is the worst tragedy you have ever heard of? Discuss with someone else the causes of that tragedy from the point of view of each person it touched. How could that calamity have been different if each person had been an ambassador of reconciliation before and after the tragedy?

4. Where is God? This is the most common question asked when tragedy strikes. How would you answer it?

5. Do you believe that God violates our freedom of choice? (Some people look at the tragedies of life—events like the Holocaust—and say that God is bad because humanity is bad.)

6. God wants us to develop our whole personality—body, mind, and soul—to show the image of God in us. How could the image of God be an integrating factor in our personalities and relationships with others?

# CHAPTER 10

## The Struggle for Faith

"Doctor, a friend of mine told me that I would have been healed if I had had enough faith. I went to a 'miracle healing service,' was prayed for, and was told I was healed. When the minister shouted 'Be healed!' a spine-tingling jolt of electricity shot through my body from head to toe. Yet by the time I returned home, the pain of my sickness began again. I felt utterly abandoned by God. The pain has shattered what faith I still had."

As my patient explained his desperate situation to me, I asked myself the obvious question, "How does one come to possess enough faith for healing?" Many people say the faithful should "claim healing" all the time. One should never doubt that he or she is being healed, for that would be a denial of faith. "Stand on the biblical promises for healing," they say. "Pray and proclaim that you are healed and you will be." Many people who have had a deep faith, however, have not been healed. Plainly, faith must be more than magical words we say in private to God or in public to other people. It must be an openness to God and a deep trusting commitment to Him as Lord and Savior in the face of defeat or tragedy.

Some patients find a deeper faith when they endure a difficult illness and struggle daily to survive. There are those, however, who fear a deep relationship with God. They think that if they commit their lives to Him, He will remove their individuality. Such people struggle against making a commitment to God, not recognizing that their circumstances can serve as a testing ground for a deep faith in Christ. Can we learn to trust Him enough in life to have confidence in Him for eternity?

Faith in Jesus Christ comes as we completely entrust our lives to Him. We rely on Him to know who we are and who we can become. We rely on Him to lead us and guide us. When I began my surgical training, Christ stimulated and inspired me and gave me the courage to become the surgeon He knew I could be. On my own I did not believe I could even get into medical school. But I had to make the effort. God could not do that for me. Now, as a surgeon, I can see that God knew what was best for me and was working in all things for my good.

Merely coping with problems and tragedies is not enough. We need to go beyond any trial by using it for growth and development. We need to communicate with God. Growth depends on our willingness to struggle. God does not operate us like robots. He does not force or shove us into trusting and depending on Him. If He wanted us to trust Him regardless of our will, He could have forced His will on human beings in the Garden of Eden.

If we seek His help and ask for His guidance as we experience life's difficulties, we respond to His love for us and demonstrate our love for Him. He allows us the freedom to turn to Him or away from Him. He gives us ample time in every situation to clarify our honest desire and ask for His help before He extends His infinite resources to us. As we talk with God, we seek an inner cleansing.

We see David doing that in the Psalms: ". . . wash me, and I shall be whiter than snow. . . . Create in me a clean heart, O God, and put a new and right spirit within me"

# The Struggle for Faith

(51:7,10). Paul says that God disciplines us for our good, and that discipline yields righteousness to those who have been trained by it (see Heb. 12:10).

Discipline means much more than just obedience to strict orders or rules. For instance, when I started my surgical residency at the University of Cincinnati, the training program centered on open dialogue with the professors. The freedom of that dynamic relationship between us allowed me to grow as a surgeon.

Dr. William A. Altemeier, my chief, told me and showed me how *he* practiced surgery. Yet when he saw patients with me, he asked me how *I* had uncovered the symptoms and signs of their disease. I had to explain how I diagnosed the patient's disease and how I planned to treat him or her. Dr. Altemeier then asked me to support my diagnosis and treatment plans with information I had gained from textbooks, journals, surgical conferences, and conversations with professors. Sometimes he accepted my work at that point, but often he gave me more instruction and knowledge. Frequently he challenged my work. Then I had to defend my treatment of the patient and decide how strongly I believed in my diagnosis and treatment plan.

That type of training sharpened my surgical judgment. Dr. Altemeier could have dictated every step of the workup and treatment of patients and forced me to obey him completely. I would have done excellent work. But he trained me through open dialogue, and the dynamic tension of our discourses led to my greater growth as a surgeon.

Another significant thing happened through that type of training program. I learned a lot about my professors—their devotion and commitment to serving patients. I developed a solid basis on which to develop my devotion and commitment to my patients. My faith in Dr. Altemeier as teacher grew deeper each year. By the end of my residency, when I had to have a major operation, I was willing to trust him with my life.

Somewhat similarly, we can use the problems of life as a training program, with Christ as our chief. But in order for that to happen we need confidence in Him and continuing commitment to Him.

*The Process of Pain*

In the past twenty years I have observed in my patients a process many people go through when they experience an illness or tragedy.

*Step one* I call the *awareness of God.* The most common question patients ask at this stage is, "God, where are You? If You are here, give me a sign; give me something that will let me be sure You are with me." Even the strongest Christian may utter those words, not as words of doubt and loneliness but as the first signs of a deepening faith. When our usual good health disappears, we are shaken. We find ourselves seeking to reestablish our relationship with God. What does it mean to be sick? Has God forsaken us? Is our faith weak? Isn't God hearing our prayers?

C. S. Lewis asked those questions when he sought to understand why his wife had died.

> Where is God? When you are happy, so happy that you have no sense of needing Him, so happy that you are tempted to feel His claim upon you as an interruption, if you remember yourself and turn to Him with gratitude and praise, you will be—or so it feels—welcomed with open arms. But go to Him when your need is desperate, when all other help is vain, and what do you find? A door slammed in your face, and a sound of bolting and double bolting on the inside. After that, silence. You may as well turn away. The longer you wait, the more emphatic the silence will

become. There are no lights in the windows. It might be an empty house. Was it ever inhabited? It seemed so once.[17]

Those questions plague us and make us wonder if our faith in God is worthwhile. Another patient asked, "Why should I believe in Him when my prayers fall on deaf ears?" Those patients who have not been aware of God before their illness often never find Him. The misery of their affliction overwhelms them too much for them to consider that He is there. Those who have a good relationship with God, who have encountered Him often in their lives before, quickly encounter Him again. Such patients then move on to the level of the presence of God. They do not question the reality of His being or His awareness of their need.

Step two is *acknowledgment of the presence of Christ* in our lives. Here patients no longer search agonizingly for Him but rejoice at every expression they see of Him. As we "practice His presence," we find our faith in Him reaffirmed.

T. Franklin Miller, a long-time friend and patient of mine, described how he practiced the presence of God during a life-threatening heart attack.

I called to my mind the five most beautiful places I have visited, the five most glorious sunsets, the five most amazing sunrises that my eyes have beheld. Then my mind turned to the five most inspiring hymns—especially the song, "Whether I live or die, whether I wake or sleep, I am the Lord's I know." I tried to think of the five most inspiring sermons that I had heard, the five most beautiful and meaningful worship services in which I had taken part, the five people who meant the most to me.[18]

Each of those memories helped Franklin strengthen his sense of the presence of God in his life.

Other patients practice God's presence by recalling that

vivid, life-changing encounter with Him when after confessing their sins and receiving God's forgiveness, they entered into a new life. I recalled my conversion when my daughter Kay Lynne was almost dead, twenty-four hours after her birth.

"God, I know you are present in this world," I exclaimed. "You came into my life when I was ten years old at the Boyertown youth camp. I knelt in the sawdust at the altar in front of the old tabernacle. With tears in my eyes and sorrow in my heart, I asked You to forgive me my sins and to give me a new and right spirit. And You did! You removed my load of sin and guilt. When I stood up and walked away from that altar, I thought I was a foot taller, and I felt as if I were walking on a cloud. I know You were there then. And since You promised never to leave me nor forsake me, I am convinced You are here with me now."

A minister once said, "When I began to regain my bearings after my heart attack, the concern I had for people returned. Once again I perceived God's presence as a strong impetus to continue my ministry."

Leon Bloy identified another evidence of God's presence when he remarked, "Joy is the most infallible sign of the presence of God."

Lawrence Brooks, who had undergone cancer surgery, expressed his certainty of the presence of God as a "wonderful, undisturbed joy."

Others have felt a deep, abiding peace that calmed their fears and soothed their anxieties. When tragedy strikes and those indicators we use for feeling His presence are weakened or seemingly gone, we have only to relive in our minds those precious times that He has been unmistakenly present with us and rest in the promises of His Word.

When our struggle of faith rests solidly on the presence of

the Lord, we can move on to the *third step: vulnerability to Jesus.* If our illness continues to worsen, we realize its energy-draining effects and begin to recognize our inability to control or correct our disease. As we call on Christ to help us, we admit our dependence on Him. One of my patients exclaimed, "O Lord, I must have Your help! If I'm ever going to get well, You will have to touch my body. I want You to guide me and help me."

Our openness to Christ usually broadens when our trials worsen. Finally, we may completely lay ourselves open to God, confessing our inner struggles, weaknesses, and need for Him. As we expose our innermost being, God can begin to work with us. He becomes, then, the solid Rock upon which we anchor our faith, just as Isaiah said, "Trust in the LORD for ever, for the LORD GOD is an everlasting rock" (Is. 26:4).

Suffering brings us to an identity crisis: Who am I? Do I want to remain the person I used to be before my tragedy, or do I want to be a better person? In the depths of our pain the restrictions and pressures of external forces on our behavior are overshadowed. As a result, suffering can produce an inner freedom. If we decide not to change, we fail to add a deeper meaning to our life. If we desire to grow, Christ will help us. He can give us not only a vision of who we can become but also the inspiration and strength to become that person.

The apostle Paul expressed his faith in Christ like this: ". . . I know whom I have believed, and am convinced that he is able to guard what I have entrusted to him for that day" (2 Tim. 1:12 NIV). The step of vulnerability to Christ's Spirit strengthens our faith, which allows us to rise above our tragedies. Vulnerability to God is a necessary step as we face our own limitations and imperfections. It is the dialogue, the communion we have with Jesus Christ, that ultimately makes our faith in Him unshakable.

After three years of suffering—a massive heart attack, gall bladder disease, and cancer of the prostate—Franklin Miller said:

Perhaps the greatest and most meaningful experience of the past three years has been the heart attack. The gall bladder disease and operation and the prostatic cancer reemphasized and amplified the wholeness that matured in me during my heart attack. I find with each new experience a deeper, more satisfying, and more successful relationship with God and His Holy Spirit. Assuredly, I still feel the anxieties of life as a human being. On the one hand, I am much more cognizant of my physical health, which requires attention and time each day to keep it in the best condition, in order that God's healing processes may be complete and worthwhile. On the other hand, I find a stronger, deeper, more compelling pull toward the development of wholeness of my total personality that someday I might be ready to live with God through eternity.

The struggles, tragedies, and victories of life have given me an unqualified, unreserved conviction that through Jesus Christ my Lord, God loves me. He is working for my good that I might be the best and most complete Christian human being that I can be.

Gratitude continues to overwhelm me for God's goodness and graciousness toward me. I no longer worry about many of the problems of life but approach those problem areas with confidence that Christ will be present and direct me, that His glorious love and mercy might be shown to a world suffering with sickness, tragedy, and death. My fear of death is much relieved. Now I experience more strongly the will to live, not only on this earth but through eternity, for I have found in Him life abundant.

The *fourth step* comes when we turn our attention more to God and His will than to ourselves. I call this *sharing in God's healing ministry*. At this level we ask Him how we can share our maturing faith in Him with the world, whether we are healed or not. Some people have expressed their deepening life of faith by helping others who will be or are facing a tragedy similar to theirs. Barbara Clausen (Chapter 6) is doing this.

Others serve people by helping them to grow and enjoy life in their present circumstances. Carl Erskine, former pitcher for the Brooklyn and Los Angeles Dodgers, helps mentally retarded children like his youngest son Jimmy to enjoy sports. He works with these children in a Special Olympics program which allows each child to compete in sports at his or her own level.

*Dynamic Faith*

Someone might say at this point that, when a person finds that God's will for him or her is serving others, the struggle for faith is over. But it isn't. Faith is never an achievement or something we obtain because we've earned it. Faith always calls us beyond ourselves into the unknown, to higher planes of living.

Just when we say "I have faith enough," we will likely encounter another experience that may threaten to overwhelm our faith. Then the struggle begins anew. Granted, we may find ourselves on firmer ground because of the faith we had before, but the new challenge may be more difficult. Yet if we continue to struggle, we will find that our faith does assure us of what we've hoped and contended for.

E. Stanley Jones had a stroke at the age of eighty-seven. Later, when he was again able, he wrote:

Now I must apply what I have been preaching through the years: that no matter what happens to us, the final result depends on how we take it.

Here I was to be called upon to illustrate and apply the Good

News, the Divine Yes, in the face of the bad news life often offers: a No. Can two more contradictory things be wrapped up into one event? Can contribution come out of collapse? In the Christian faith can it still be the Divine Yes, no matter what happens? But to accept a commission such as the Divine Yes the greatest problem lies in the one who accepts it. He must be convinced that the Divine Yes is not only possible, but will sustain one and supply his or her every need.

You can't play verbal tricks on yourself; you must really believe it. This can't be an example of trying harder, of whipping up the will. No matter how honest and dedicated, the human will knows its own weaknesses and limitations.[19]

There are other notable examples of people who have found a specific calling in God's healing ministry. One of these is Elisabeth Elliot. Her husband and four other men were killed in Ecuador by the Auca Indians, whom they were serving as missionaries. She responded to that tragedy by living among the Aucas herself, loving them and bringing the love of Christ to them.[20]

Charles Colson is another person whose faith in Jesus Christ has turned tragedy into a personal triumph. Out of his implication in the Watergate scandal and subsequent imprisonment he has gone on to found a ministry to prisoners throughout the country.[21]

Many others have found that their tragedies have given opportunity for God to reveal Himself in transformation and help.

Joni Eareckson, a young artist, broke her neck in a diving accident at the age of seventeen. She has described her struggle for faith in Jesus Christ and her desire to be useful even though she is a quadriplegic: "At first I drew for fun," she said, "then, to occupy my time; finally to express my feelings for what God was doing in me. Now my art is a reflection of how God can empower someone like me to rise above circumstances."[22]

Each of these people responded to God in a way directly related to his or her own tragedy. Although most people will not be able to respond so directly for various reasons, there is, nevertheless, another way that everyone can share in God's healing ministry. That is through the ministry of reconciliation. To paraphrase Albert Schweitzer: And through those whom He indwells, whether they be simple or wise, He will reveal Himself in the relationships they have, in the fellowship with the suffering and hurting people they serve. And as an ineffable mystery those served shall see the image of God in His servants.

**For Discussion**

1. How do *you* increase your faith in Jesus Christ? Do your beliefs about the creation of this world hinder or help your faith?

2. Think of two or three experiences that have increased your faith in God. Then examine those experiences to see why your faith increased. Was your faith strengthened because you actually saw signs of His presence or because you had a deeper relationship with Him? Did those experiences provide you with greater strength for your next trial?

3. How do you respond to the concept that faith is a struggle to believe that Christ is Lord and that He will provide the resources we need to grow beyond our tragedies if we trust Him?

4. Where does *your* faith come from: reading the Word? family environment? other people's personal experience? the faithfulness of God in *your* trials and sufferings?

5. Recount the growth of your own faith over the past ten years or since you became a Christian. What has been the major emphasis of that faith? How much further are you in your faith in Christ now than you were?

6. In the first part of this chapter I described the "open dialogue" discipline of my surgical training. Contrast such an approach to faith with the passive faith of some Christians. Does "trusting Christ" allow for laziness?

7. Try to express to another person how dialogue with Christ in your present problems can strengthen your belief in your ultimate resurrection.

8. Look back at the last problem or time of suffering that you have gone through. Examine it by using the steps of faith described in this chapter.

9. How have you shared in God's healing ministry? Have you carried that ministry into your everyday life?

# CHAPTER 11

## From Here to Eternity: A Conclusion

Francis A. Schaeffer has written, "When we were created, we were created for a purpose. And the purpose of our creation, in which all our subsidiary purposes fit, is to be in a personal relationship to God, in communion with Him, in love, by choice, the creature before the Creator."[23]

Only the human being, out of all earth's creatures, is given responsibility for developing into the creature he or she was created to be. I have seen some of my patients grow and mature despite their suffering. Why was this true of some but not of others? Those who grew were patients who chose not to remain primarily interested in their bodies but to go beyond the physical to the spiritual. They saw *their* responsibility to become what God created them to be: spiritually centered beings, God's companions.

In *Escape From Evil*, Ernest Becker concluded, "To finish one's personality is to respond to faith which asks man to expand himself trustingly, to transcend himself in God and find meaning for his existence in God."[24]

Having faith in God did not come easily for any of the people whose cases I described in Part One. Yet faith provides spiritual expansion so that the storms of life can crash down on us but not destroy us. After these patients had worked through their doubt and fear, they were able to find wholeness of personality in Jesus Christ.

We, too, need to struggle for faith in order to be sure that we truly desire to commune with God. How else can we be certain that we will enjoy living with God for eternity if we haven't proven to ourselves in this life that God is our primary source of joy?

Many people whose lives I touch relate to God as they do to me—as a therapist who will cure their ills. Often they are people who have given time and money to God's cause. When they suffer, they feel that it is God's turn to help them. Leslie D. Weatherhead was disturbed by that kind of attitude.

> I am often troubled by the querulous people who come to me in some distress or another and say, "I have prayed to God and I do trust God." "I've gone to church all my life . . . and I say my prayers night and morning." . . . They have made no serious quest to get into that joyous relationship with God of the child to the loving father. They want God as they want anything—a tonic, or an operation, or any other kind of treatment would do which would give them health or ease.[25]

Unless such people change their attitude and give their sufferings to Christ, they will not be able to deal adequately with their pain. Ultimately my patients who are seeking and growing develop a steadfast faith, unshaken not only by the problems of life but by the inevitability of their own death.

### Toward Understanding Death

We can learn from our serious problems something helpful about death. As Christians we can be certain that physical death does not end human existence. Many times I have seen people die. All of us must die. But Christ's resurrection assures us that death is not the end of life. An awareness of death can encourage us to make more of our lives now. How can we find meaning in the fact of death?

Most of my patients begin by fearing death. When suffering strips people of their energies and abilities, they often wonder if they are about to die. They begin to question why they have lived, of what value their life has been, and whether they have succeeded in becoming the person they were created to be. Out of that questioning comes a strong motivation to reexamine their lives and reorder their priorities. Many patients have told me that their sufferings have caused them to reevaluate past attitudes and actions.

Death itself is irreversible. When we die, who we have been and what we have done will stand forever. God will judge us on the choices we have made. What will God see as the center of our lives? What has been the "delight of our soul?"

Life is unrepeatable. If death were not a part of life, perhaps we would choose forever to reject God's love and concern for us. We would be too interested in the "status quo" to change.

I have found that most patients are not ready when death comes. Therefore, we need to question *now* what we are doing with our lives. Can I love and respect myself in view of the person I have been? Who or what have I served and lived for? As Paul Tournier says, "Underlying every decisive choice there is a prior, fundamental choice, a spiritual one, the choice of one's God: What is your God? Your mother, your own self-interests, your instincts, your pleasure, reason, science, or Jesus Christ?"[26]

When we think about such questions we sharpen our self-image. Do we want to stay as we are or do we want to grow?

"Has my life been worthwhile?" That question pursues us throughout our lives until we come to grips with the implications of our mortality. Ernest Becker comments:

Man wants to know that his life has somehow counted, if not for himself, then at least in a larger scheme of things, that it has left a trace, a trace that has meaning. Or, if there is to be a "final" tally of the scurrying of man on earth—a "judgment day"—then this trace of one's life must enter that tally and put on record who one was and that what one did was significant.[27]

All of us want to tie the loose strings of life together and know that our life has had a purpose, direction, goal. In fact, many physical illnesses result from the inner distress produced by the meaninglessness people find in their lives. Jesus Christ says we can find the highest meaning and purpose for life if we seek first the kingdom of God (see Matt. 6:33). Do we believe Him?

God calls us to live a holy life. The prophet Micah said, ". . .' and what does the LORD require of you but to do justice, and to love kindness, and to walk humbly with your God?' " (Mic. 6:8). Jesus Christ tells us that ". . . whoever desires to save his life will lose it, and whoever loses his life for my sake will find it" (Matt. 16:25 NKJB-NT). Christians not only have their own standard by which they measure the success of their lives, but they recognize that God has a requirement as well. If we fail to achieve God's measure for our lives, we fail as human beings to find fulfillment. We die defeated. "So God created man in his own image . . . ; male and female created he them" (Gen. 1:27). It is this potential, the image of God in which we have been created, that makes us unique.

### Beyond Death's Door

What evidence do we have that there is life beyond the grave? To begin with, God has made our world in such a way that we have abundant opportunities to find Him. He has planted evidence throughout nature for us to see His sovereignty. Year after year, nature rehearses the themes of death and immortality through the seasons. Just as plants and trees seem to die in the dead of winter and then suddenly burst forth with new life and growth in the springtime, so we can gain confidence that we too will live after the dead winter season of our lives.

Journalist Lincoln Barnett states in *The Universe and Dr. Einstein*, "In the evolution of scientific thought, one fact has become impressively clear: there is no mystery of the physical world which does not point to a mystery beyond itself."[28] Man's inescapable impasse, according to Barnett, is that he himself is part of the world he seeks to explore. Therefore the only world we can truly know is the world created for us by our senses. Moreover, what we know outside our senses we have only representations of; we have to make some assumptions about those representations. For instance, we do not actually see individual stars that are outside our galaxy; yet we have evidence of their existence beyond the limits of our senses.

A Christian perspective, however, embraces more than evidences in our physical world that point to life beyond our senses. We have the Word of God, the Bible, and its recorded accounts of Jesus' raising people from the dead: a widow's son, a little girl, Lazarus. As our supreme example we point to Jesus' death and resurrection. He said, ". . .' I am the resurrection and the life; he who believes in me, though he die, yet shall he live, and whoever lives and believes in me shall never die . . .' " (John 11:25). Through faith in Jesus Christ, we have hope for eternity.

But now Christ is risen from the dead, and has become the firstfruits of those who have fallen asleep. For since by man came death, by Man also came the resurrection of the dead. For as in

Adam all die, even so in Christ all will be made alive. But each one in his own order: Christ the firstfruits, afterward those who are Christ's at His coming.

Behold, I tell you a mystery: We shall not all sleep, but we shall all be changed—in a moment, in the twinkling of an eye, at the last trumpet. For the trumpet will sound, and the dead will be raised incorruptible, and we shall be changed. For this corruptible must put on incorruption, and this mortal must put on immortality. So when this corruptible has put on incorruption, and this mortal has put on immortality, then shall be brought to pass the saying that is written: "Death is swallowed up in victory."
"O death, where is your sting?
O Hades, where is your victory?"
. . . But thanks be to God, who gives us the victory through our Lord Jesus Christ. Therefore, my beloved brethren, be steadfast, immovable, always abounding in the work of the Lord, inasmuch as you know that your labor is not in vain in the Lord (1 Cor. 15:20-23; 51-55; 57,58 NKJB-NT).

When my grandfather was dying, he called my dad to his side and said, "Good-bye, my Master calls." Then he raised his hand and stopped breathing.

Jesus is our hope of eternity. When we have had a deep personal relationship with Him through life, we can trust Him in our death.

*For Discussion*
1. What does death mean to you physically, psychologically, spiritually?

2. Have you had an experience in which you have come close to death? What did you learn from that experience? Did it change your life's goals or cause you to set new

priorities or attitudes? If you have not had such an experience, talk to someone who has.

3. What response can you make to someone who says there is no resurrection of the dead?

4. Someone has said that when we are ready to die, we are ready to live. What do you consider worth dying for (and therefore worth living for)?

5. The apostle Paul, in Romans 8:35, asked "Who shall separate us from the love of Christ? . . ." Read again Romans 8:35–39. Do you think that Paul's suffering for Christ developed his faith enough that he could trust Christ even in death? Why? Have you come to the same conclusion through your own sufferings?

6. Since we have weak, mortal bodies, how can we show the power of God in our lives? Recall in your mind some instances when the power of Christ in you was unmistakable.

## NOTES
1. Eugenia Price, *No Pat Answers* (Grand Rapids: Zondervan, 1972), pp. 11–12, 129.
2. James Angel, *O Susan* (Anderson, Ind.: Warner Press, 1973), p. 36.
3. Albert Schweitzer, *The Quest of the Historical Jesus* (New York: MacMillan, 1948), p. 403.
4. Angel, *O Susan*, p. 37.
5. Annie Johnson Flint, *Hymns for the Family of God* (Nashville: Paragon Associates, Inc., 1976), p. 112.
6. *Webster's New Collegiate Dictionary* (Chicago: Doubleday and Co., 1978), p. 1326.
7. Paul Tournier, *A Doctor's Casebook in the Light of the Bible*, Jubilee edition (New York: Harper and Row, 1976), p. 119.
8. Ibid., pp. 113–14.
9. Malcolm A. Jeeves, *The Scientific Enterprise and Christian Faith* (Downers Grove, Ill.: InterVarsity Press, 1971), pp. 21–22.
10. C. S. Lewis, *Miracles: A Preliminary Study* (New York: MacMillan, 1947), p. 112.
11. David Elton Trueblood, *Philosophy of Religion* (Grand Rapids: Baker Book House, 1975), pp. 209–10.
12. John Sutherland Bonnell, *Do You Want to be Healed?* (New York: Harper and Row, 1968), p. 157.
13. Dietrich Bonhoeffer, *Christ the Center* (New York: Harper and Row, 1960), pp. 115–16.
14. Ibid., pp. 114–15.
15. Price, *No Pat Answers*, pp. 120, 124.

16. Lloyd J. Ogilvie, *Let God Love You* (Waco, Texas: Word Books, 1974), pp. 13, 78.
17. C. S. Lewis, *A Grief Observed* (New York: The Seabury Press, 1976), pp. 4–5.
18. T. Franklin Miller, personal communication, 1976.
19. E. Stanley Jones, *The Divine Yes* (Nashville: Abingdon, 1976), pp. 33–34.
20. Elisabeth Elliot, *Through Gates of Splendor* (New York: Harper Brothers, 1957).
21. Charles Colson, *Born Again* (Old Tappen, N.J.: Fleming H. Revell, 1977), pp. 342–44.
22. Joni Eareckson, *Joni* (Grand Rapids: Zondervan, 1976), pp. 206, 215.
23. Francis A. Schaeffer, *True Spirituality* (Wheaton, Ill.: Tyndale House, 1971), p. 88.
24. Ernest Becker, *Escape from Evil* (New York: The Free Press, 1975), p. xvii.
25. Leslie D. Weatherhead, *Why Do Men Suffer?* (New York: Abingdon, 1936), p. 183.
26. Paul Tournier, *The Meaning of Persons* (New York: Harper and Row, 1957), p. 209.
27. Becker, *Escape*, p. 4.
28. Lincoln Barnett, *The Universe and Dr. Einstein* (New York: The New American Library of World Literature, 1952), p. 127.

CPSIA information can be obtained at www.ICGtesting.com
Printed in the USA
BVOW011838110912

300158BV00002B/2/P

9 781622 308262